Doubting is difficult, but the real threat to faith is doubting alone. Christin Taylor's new book, *Crew*, offers a surprisingly radical, practical, and countercultural call to Christian hospitality in a world stuck in isolation. For those with upturned lives or overturned dreams, it is a guide back into what you were striving for all along, had you known: authentic Christian community.

— DAVID DRURY, chief of staff of The Wesleyan Church; author and coauthor
of half a dozen books, including *Being Dad* and *SoulShift*

If this book is about finding one's crew, then I want Christin Taylor in my boat. Her words, anecdotes, and research are a map through the choppy waters of guiding others — and ourselves — through life's transitions. Taylor draws readers in, not with simplistic solutions, but rather by offering vivid stories of transformation. She demonstrates that healing can only come when one fully embraces his or her own journey partnered with community. This book is a treasure and tool for young adults, parents, pastors, and mentors seeking wisdom on how to navigate the inevitable shifts life presents.

— KRISTIN RITZAU, author of *A Beautiful Mess*,
adjunct faculty member at Azusa Pacific University

Christin Taylor weaves a powerful tapestry of the challenges of young adulthood. More importantly, she brings to life the concepts of learning partnerships and good company for young adults' developmental journeys. Authentically sharing her own experiences and deepest thoughts and emotions, she portrays the nature of good company in ways readers can see in their own lives. She balances a deep sensitivity to adults' — particularly parents' — struggles to offer the space for younger adults to grow and the imperative that the space is essential. She not only offers a rich description of the good company she advocates; she embodies the principles of good company in her writing. This book will be good company for young adults who are making their way into adulthood as well as those who are trying to accompany them.

— MARCIA BAXTER MAGOLDA, author of *Authoring Your Life*

Finding your way in a sea of opposition can be one of the greatest struggles encountered in life. In *Crew*, Christin Taylor guides readers through the process of overcoming the hurdles and challenges that exist on this journey. Filled with vulnerable stories of how she overcame these same struggles, Taylor shares a simple yet effective approach to opening our lives, and the freedom that comes in trusting in community. If you've ever felt misguided, alone, or afraid of how to go on, this is the book for you.

—JEREMY SUMMERS, coauthor of *Awakening Grace*,
director of spiritual formation for The Wesleyan Church

Christin Taylor is one of those rare writers able to draw insight and wisdom from her own experience, and to communicate life lessons through riveting personal narrative. Her language is direct, uncluttered, mercifully free of cleverness, and entirely fresh. If you are looking for genuine inspiration, presented in a wonderfully humble voice, then this is the book, which is about thriving in that face of adversity, is for you. Taylor *listens* as she speaks, a skill that allows a higher voice to flow into her writing.

—DUSTIN BEALL SMITH, author of
Key Grip: A Memoir of Endless Consequences

CREW

FINDING COMMUNITY
WHEN YOUR DREAMS CRASH

CHRISTIN N. TAYLOR

wphonline.com

Copyright © 2014 by Christin Taylor
Published by Wesleyan Publishing House
Indianapolis, Indiana 46250
Printed in the United States of America
ISBN: 978-0-89827-707-4
ISBN (e-book): 978-0-89827-708-1

Library of Congress Cataloging-in-Publication Data

Taylor, Christin N.
  Crew : finding community when your dreams crash / Christin Taylor.
    pages cm
  Includes bibliographical references.
  ISBN 978-0-89827-707-4
  1. Fellowship--Religious aspects--Christianity. 2. Suffering--Religious
aspects--Christianity. I. Title.
  BV4517.5.T39 2014
  248.8'4--dc23
                                    2013047216

Note: This book is based on the author's memory, journal entries, and when possible, consultation with people whose stories appear in the book. Most names have remained the same, but in some instances, names and identifying details have been changed to preserve anonymity. There are no composite characters or events in this book. Some people have been left out of the story, but only when that omission had no impact on the truth or substance of the story.

Dedicated to Ashley Hill, Emily Anne Geddes,
Molly Chrisman, and Jaqi Schaeffer

We are only fellow travelers—at different places on the road,

perhaps, but fallible and ordinary nonetheless.

—Margaret Guenther

CONTENTS

ACKNOWLEDGEMENTS

I couldn't do what I do without the incredible support of my own crew—my family. Dwayne, you are a life-partner out of my dreams. Noelle and Nathan, you make life worth writing about.

Special thanks to my mentor and friend, Dr. Mary Brown. Mary, you have walked with me through this journey of writing from my earliest days. Thank you for your honest feedback and your hours of investment into me and my writing. You are as much responsible for my career, as anyone else I can think of.

Thank you to Kevin Scott and the fabulous team at Wesleyan Publishing House. Thank you for believing in me, for making my books readable, and for giving me this incredible opportunity to write professionally.

Finally, to all the young adults at Western Washington University, who have trusted me with their stories and let me join them for parts of their journey. You all have inspired me, and taught me what it means to be good company.

Introduction

THE LONG ROAD TO BELLINGHAM

The long arm of dawn curled somewhere behind the horizon, not yet ready to touch the morning pink. I stood on the sidewalk wrapped in a quiet I seldom heard in Los Angeles. Everyone was in bed by now. At 3:30 a.m., even the partiers, divas, musicians, artisans, and bohemians were unwinding into sleep. Over me the silhouette of a lone palm tree arched against the slate sky. Dwayne pushed another suitcase into the corner of the back seat, the dome lights muted by the piles of boxes and bags already filling every blank space.

"Are we ready to get Noelle?" I asked, my voice hushed into the creases of that strange hour—not quite night and not quite morning. Even though Dwayne and I had been up since midnight going over every last detail of our long move up the coast, my body jumped with adrenaline. Just three hours before, I folded my outfit for the first day on the road into a neat pile beside the suitcases. Dwayne and I rehearsed the order in which we would do everything the next morning, keeping our voices low so as not to wake my cousins in the next room. We would get up, dress, put the bags in the car, then, finally, get the most precious cargo of all: lift Noelle carefully out of her Pak 'n Play, and tuck her into the car seat as seamlessly as possible so as not to wake her.

We were leaving at 3:30 in the morning because it would take twelve hours to drive up the spine of California. This was just the first of a three-day journey from Southern California to Bellingham, Washington, the last big city before the Canadian border. Some friends of ours, who have three kids of their own, advised us to leave early in the morning, while Noelle was still asleep. "That way, she'll sleep for the first three hours of the trip," my friend said.

Dwayne looked around the empty driveway of my cousin's house. Our eyes met for a moment in the hush of that in-between hour, and he nodded.

Inside the house, every room was still. I padded my way back down the hallway to the guest room where Dwayne and I had stayed the first night we moved to L.A., seven years earlier. So much had changed since then.

I pushed open the door to see the shadow of the Pak 'n Play wedged up to the foot of our bed. Seven years ago, Dwayne and I slept in that bed as a newly married couple, just twenty-one and twenty-two. Now here we were with a two-year-old, making another cross-country move. Only this time we weren't leaving the home our parents had built for us, we were leaving the home we had built for ourselves.

I slid my hands as smoothly as possible beneath the warm lump of my daughter's body and lifted. I touched her gently to my shoulder, trying to glide over the carpet, but in three steps, she was awake. She blinked and lifted her warm cheek off my shoulder, immediately alert.

I buckled her into the car seat, reassuring myself that she would fall asleep once we started driving. This was going to be one long ride if we had to keep her entertained from the dark hours of the morning to the rosy hours of evening.

"Is that everything?" Dwayne asked as we buckled ourselves in. I looked out the window at my cousin's house. They had let us stay with them for our last night in L.A., since the majority of our belongings were purged, sold, and given away. What was left had been puzzled inside our U-haul trailer.

I took a deep breath and turned back toward him. "That's everything." Taking each other's hands, we pulled out into that gray hour, saying good-bye to our friends, our family, our city, and our twenties.

Los Angeles was not just the city where we lived after graduating from college; it was the city where we shipwrecked. It was the city where we crashed into the waves of adulthood, shattered like debris, and gradually floated onto the golden sands of home. As we hauled our trailer up the Grapevine, I looked back at the grand basin where my life had pooled and reshaped over the last seven years.

Sharon Daloz Parks says in her book *Big Questions, Worthy Dreams* that most everyone hits a metaphorical shipwreck in their twenties.[1] This is an event, big or small, subtle or not, that rips apart the very fabric of our identity. Shipwreck can be triggered by any number of things. It can happen because we don't get the job we want, a significant relationship falls apart, we experience physical illness or injury, or we discover an intellectual construct no longer works for us. Regardless of the cause of shipwreck, the result is the same: calling into question everything we think we know about ourselves, the world, and God. It threatens us in a total and primal way.

Dwayne and I had both experienced our shipwrecks in L.A. Mine had to do with working in the film industry: a career that shattered me and forced me to look deep inside my own motivations, my own sense of self. I was a shadow of a girl living to prove herself to the world through what I perceived as success and mission. What I learned instead was that I would always be a shadow of a girl if any part of my identity and future was built by my own hands. Instead, I learned to trust a God whom C. S. Lewis described, via his picture of Aslan, as wild but good—a God I could not pin down, could not predict, but was forced nonetheless to trust despite the wreck he led me into.[2] In the end, I found a future—an identity fuller, richer, deeper, and more authentic than any I could have bought, borrowed, or scraped together on my own.

All of this coming apart and pulling back together again happened in the hands of some very wise and beautiful people. I felt the air leave my lungs every time I imagined leaving them behind in the sun and grit of L.A.—Erika, Drew, Melissa, Lynn, David, Jeff, Amy, Teresa, Kristin. The names trotted out from my heart like streamers chasing our car north. How would I find my way forward without these people in my life anymore? I watched as the hills swallowed them up, tucking them behind peak after peak.

In her book *Authoring Your Life*, Marcia Baxter Magolda writes that when we move from adolescence to young adulthood, a shift happens in the hierarchies of our life.[3] Whereas our parents, teachers, and coaches once sat on the front of the tandem bike leading our way, guiding us through tough decisions, now, the steering is up to us. They must get off the bike and take their seats behind us. We move forward and take the handlebars. We still need them in our lives, but we need them in a separate faculty other than authority. Baxter Magolda calls this being good company — a theory that has been adopted by universities across the country as they seek to educate their students both in- and outside the classroom.

Indeed, when I was living in L.A., clawing my way through some of the darkest days of my life, it was Erika, Drew, Jeff, Amy, and all the names I listed above who had sat on the back of my bike and given me forward momentum, all the while allowing me to learn who I was and how to be an adult.

We were moving to Bellingham now, because Dwayne took a position as a resident director at Western Washington University. I was just thirty years old, he was twenty-nine, both on the cusp of a new decade of our lives. We were turning toward a new, more committed phase of life. Dwayne had finally found a career he loved in student affairs, I was teaching and writing, and we were planning on expanding our family soon.

In so many ways, my shipwreck felt behind me, though its ripples were still present in my life. In so many ways, I felt like an adult, as if we were finally starting life, the chaos and scramble and transition of young adulthood behind us. It was time for us to invest in our family and our careers, which were both dedicated to working with college students and young adults. It was time for us to move from being young adults ourselves in need of good company, to thirtysomethings offering good company to the young adults in our backyard.

I mean "backyard" almost literally. As a resident director, Dwayne was provided a two-bedroom apartment on the second floor of Edens Hall, a grand building perched on the side of an arboretum and facing out toward the Puget Sound. Below our window, the rest of the campus of Western Washington University unfurled into the downtown of Bellingham, which likewise unfurled into the bay. The students lived above and all around us. They paced back and forth outside our door. We rode the elevator with them, ate dinners in the dining hall with them, and took long walks in the evening all around campus with Noelle speeding away on her little trike hollering at all the students she knew.

Everything I've learned about being good company started during our two years in Bellingham. I watched as Dwayne and his staff implemented the learning theories of Marcia Baxter Magolda. I read and researched young adult identity development theories as I wrote my first book. Most importantly,

I hosted a steady stream of twentysomethings and college students in our apartment. I cooked dinner for them. We played games and knitted and crocheted together. We watched movies and had coffee together. But mostly we sat into the late hours of the night talking about life and the future.

As I write this book about being and finding good company, it's hard for me not to return to Western Washington University and the staff and students we met there over and over again in my mind. Story after story blooms from the page, based on the lives of these people, the insights, the education. The truth is that WWU does extraordinarily well at providing good company to its students. Their entire residential education model was based on Marcia Baxter Magolda's theory of self-authorship and the steps she proposes for walking with young adults through major transitions.

As you read this book, you'll meet many students and staff members from Western, the fertile ground where I learned most about how to be good company. We may not all be so lucky to work or live at an institution that has so methodically and carefully cultivated an environment of good partnership and has watched its students and employees flourish in response. And so, in this book, I hope to share with you just a little of what I learned there and pass along the goodness.

1

THE BUCK

I knew we weren't in Los Angeles anymore when we rounded the corner and saw a gorgeous buck blinking at us from the side of the road. He stood regal and silent; his sinewy neck arched elegantly back, his antlers framing the sky. Dwayne and I gasped in astonishment.

"Noelle, look!" I whispered, as if the buck could hear us outside the glass and metal of our vehicle. In an instant, he was gone, melting away into the thicket of dark green trees that lined the sides of the road. Amazingly, we saw this bit of wildlife on the edge of campus, in the grid of the city, not out in the wilds of Washington. We had finally arrived in Bellingham just a few minutes earlier, and were driving along the arm of road that hugged the edge of campus.

We had successfully pulled our trailer over the Grapevine and then the Sierra Nevada mountains between California and Oregon, but none of those inclines ground our engine like that one final short but steep driveway up into the parking lot of the residence hall where we would be living. Western Washington University sits on the hills above Bellingham, and our car reminded us with much groaning and choking of just how far we had come from the broad, smooth freeways of Los Angeles.

"Welcome!" a lanky man with a newsboy hat called as he took the pavement in sweeping strides toward us. Dwayne parked the car and hopped out. I tumbled out of the passenger seat crumpled and relieved to finally have arrived. "I'm John!" the man smiled and shook my hand. I knew from Dwayne's descriptions that this was Dr. John Purdie, the associate director of residence life and the man who had hired Dwayne. In other words, he was the boss.

One by one, the rest of the residence life staff strode around the corner of the building and welcomed us with open arms. I was relieved to find myself wrapped in warm hugs from people with smiling faces. Names followed the faces in a string of syllables I could barely remember: June, Jake, Hui-Ling, Dave,

Chenthu, Matt. One name in particular stuck though—Stephanie. "I'm so excited to finally meet you!" Stephanie crooned when she saw me. She gave me a big hug and her silky black hair brushed across my cheek. "If ever you need anything, just let me know. I can tell you where the grocery stores are and the best gas stations." Beneath the warmth of her smile, I felt my anxieties about making friends evaporate. Here was a friend, ready to go.

"This is where you're going to be living." John pointed up to the building beneath which we had parked. "It's the second oldest building on campus but was renovated just a few years ago." I looked up to see a broad, brick face with stately white pillars. Whitewashed steps marched to the lip of the entrance. Hugging the back of the residence hall, a massive arboretum rose to the sky, blotting out the horizon. Inside, John showed us an elegant wood staircase that curved around the wall and led to the second floor. Down the hall on the left, he slipped his key into a door and opened it to show us our new apartment.

The resident director apartment was three dorm rooms remodeled into a two bedroom apartment complete with a full kitchen. Windows stretched across the outside wall. Through the glass, leafy branches waved, touching the tops of other residence halls farther down the hill. Beyond the branches and residence halls,

I could see the wink and blink of water rippling out to the horizon. I looked up to take in the fourteen-foot ceilings. The apartment felt spacious and newly cleaned. The carpet was an industrial low-cropped blue, and the furniture provided by the school was the same shade of blue, upholstered in fire-retardant material—the kind of furniture you might find in a student lounge.

"What do you think?" Dwayne whispered as we walked from room to room. I nodded my head.

"Good," I said with a smile. We could make a home here.

Dwayne beamed as we walked around the residence hall and then out onto campus. His excitement was almost tangible. Working for a school like Western was a dream job. They had an outstanding residence life program. Using the learning theories of Marcia Baxter Magolda, John had cultivated a Residential Education Model that fell in line beautifully with everything Dwayne had been learning in graduate school. The program at Western not only groomed excellent student leaders, but also excellent student affairs professionals.

As a part of the program, every student affairs professional was required to be trained in Marcia Baxter Magolda's theory of self-authorship and good company, and each resident advisor had to begin by taking a class to learn the principles of how to be good company for their residents.

It was in this context that I became acquainted with Baxter Magolda's work and her learning-partner theory. And it was in this context, living among college students and student affairs professionals, that I started to ask a question: "What is the different between being a mentor and being good company?" On the surface these roles seem almost interchangeable. Both involve working with young adults, both denote a type of relationship that helps us navigate unknown waters, and both teach us something integral about who we are.

So, having gotten up the courage, I e-mailed Marcia my question. A few days later, I got this reply, written in Marcia's generous tone: "I think of mentoring being different [from] good company in that it has an element of hierarchy to it; whereas, good company walks side by side or even behind the young adult."

After spending the last five years living among college students and student affairs professionals and after having read and researched as many books on young adult identity development as I could find, here is what I have walked away understanding: While the mentor relationship can be a powerful one, it is something other than and different from being good company.

Essentially, mentoring is someone standing ahead of us, leading us, imparting to us some great knowledge and experience we have yet to find on our own. Carl Jung offers an archetype of the mentor as an old man who "represents knowledge, reflection, insight, wisdom, cleverness and intuition."[1] This old man appears in our lives when we need "insight, understanding, good advice, determination, planning," but can't muster these gifts on our own.[2] In other words, the mentor arrives at just the right moment to bail us out, to rescue us. The mentor is more learned, wiser, and more powerful than us. And by the mentor's power he or she can shield, protect, and guard us from ourselves. The mentor relationship is a gift in and of its own right. But it is not what this book is about.

This book is about making our own way, about finding and being good company. Good company doesn't stand in front of us or even beside us, but behind us. Good company offers us encouragement when we need it, pushes us forward when we'd like to retreat, but all the while lets us steer the proverbial ship, lets us pick and choose our own way forward. Good company does not shield, does not protect, and cannot even really light our way forward. Good company is there for another reason entirely—to help us learn who we are.

Right now, our parents, if they've happened to pick up this book, just had a heart attack. The last thing they want is for us to have full control of the ship of our life and accidentally career onto the craggy shores of life. I get this. I'm a parent now. My whole life is dedicated to protecting my children, keeping my daughter from falling out of a tree and breaking her neck, keeping my son from choking on a rubber band. Hopefully one day I'll have nurtured them well enough, led them and trained them well enough that they don't eventually self-implode. It's a weighty task and one that vexes my every moment with love and anxiety.

So I understand how terrifying the concept of good company sounds to the ears of a parent. The freedom good company lends us to make our own choices sounds like a useless and dangerous thing. And I would be lying if I said that the power we find in good company to steer our own future isn't in some way dangerous.

"My children are making decisions now with huge consequences. It doesn't always feel like they are prepared to make those decisions, but there they are—on the tightrope without a net." These words still echo in my ears. They came from a former professor of mine. A good professor and extraordinary dad. I've known him for more than ten years now and have watched his young adult children morph from scrappy kids running around the church parking lot to twentysomethings both graduated and married.

My professor openly admits that he and his wife don't much care for this phase of parenting. "As a parent, I feel as powerless as I've ever been in my parental experience." He and his wife have wrestled for the past couple years with their new role in their children's lives. They've struggled to stand on the sidelines and watch as their young adult children make choices that they don't agree with and find unwise. It's broken their hearts as they've tried to speak into their kids' lives, only to watch their advice be rejected or simply ignored.

The truth is, from the outside looking in, his kids are doing great. They're both happily married, in strong relationships, and navigating their way through their twenties with as much surety as can be expected of any of us who are wading into the waters of adulthood for the first time. Still, one child rushed quickly into marriage, and the other doesn't care much for church or faith at the moment. These decisions have made their parents reel with anxiety.

In a moment of candor, my professor lamented, "Where they were making significant decisions before, in their childhood, we were there to give counsel. But when they leave our home, the assumption is we'll mind our own business." And he's absolutely right. There is a way in which our parents have to step back and give up control in our lives when we leave home.

He's echoing Baxter Magolda's analogy of the tandem bike. He is articulating just how difficult it's been for him and his wife to move to the back seat of the bike. They no longer call the shots, or make the decisions. He's struggling to figure out just how much influence he wields in his children's lives now that he no longer has authority.

What my professor faces—what all of our parents face when they watch us go off to college and then step out into a world full of choices and mammoth risks—is an infinite sea of self-doubt and a gagging sense of fear. And the truth is, all of their fears are our fears too. What if we don't find a career? What if we marry the wrong person—or no person at all and end up alone at the end of our lives? What if we spiral down in our young adult years rather than up? What if we encounter disappointment so devastating that we shatter into irretrievable pieces? The "what-ifs" skirt the landscape of our twenties like skittish deer, calling into question everything we think we know about ourselves, the world around us, and God.

It's in the face of such uncertainty and such elusive answers, that Marcia Baxter Magolda, enters the scene and says that what we need as young adults on our journey toward ourselves is good company. Not someone to take our hands and lead us through the choppy, threatening terrain of our twenties, but someone to sit behind us, traveling with us.

How on earth could it possibly be good for us, in the face of such huge consequences, in the midst of such unwieldy hopes and dreams, with still only a bud of ourselves understood, to have someone riding behind us, letting us choose all along our own futures, our own destinies, our own heartbreaks?

That is what this book is about. So let's dive in. Let's look first at what exactly good company is, then what it is we are facing in our twenties that requires such good company. And then let us look at how we go about finding and being good company. Where can we find her? How do we get him? And how can we offer company to those closest to us?

Ultimately, the answers to these questions are not what we would expect. Or rather, they're not what we, and particularly our parents, might hope for. But they're exactly what we need. Like the elegant buck standing on the crux of the road, good company meets us in the transition between two states, two selves, signaling to us that a whole new adventure is about to begin.

2

A LESSON FROM THE BENEDICTINE BROTHERS

In the order of Saint Benedict, there is a rule that all guests should be received by the monks as if they are receiving Christ himself. As a result, there is an extraordinary culture of hospitality among the Benedictine brothers and sisters.

I've experienced this hospitality up close.

The summer that Dwayne graduated from his master's program, he and I agreed I should take a weekend away to retreat and write. We reserved a room at Prince of Peace Abbey in Oceanside, California.

That weekend, I pulled up to a large circular parking lot at the top of a hill. The abbey glistened white beneath the Southern

California sun. The blue rooftops winked down at the ocean glinting and sprawling away under the horizon. In the center of the parking lot, a white statue of Jesus towered over the hill, his face turned down in a gentle gaze, his hands outstretched saying, "Come."

I was met in the welcome house by a brother wrapped in brown folds of cloth. He carried with him an old walkman, and large headphones cupped around his neck.

"Welcome," he said, bowing his head to me. He signed me in and quietly led me back through the abbey, past a tidy foyer filled with soft chairs and shelves of books.

"The dining room is through that door," he pointed to the opposite end of the foyer. "And if you would like to eat in silence, the silent dining room is beside it." His finger shifted slightly to the right.

I nodded and heaved my overnight bag higher up onto my shoulder.

From there, he led me back out of the building to a courtyard with roses, lined on the periphery by rooms. All the doors faced inward, toward the flowers and concrete benches. We stopped at a nondescript door on the right and the brother handed me a key.

"Brother Earnest will be here shortly to welcome you," and with a small tilt of his head my guide was gone. I smiled and turned toward my room. The door slid open and I found inside a modest, bare-bones, but exquisitely clean space. A single bed was slid against the wall and already made with crisp white sheets, a pillow and warm blanket folded neatly at the end. Adjacent to the bed was a large upholstered chair and between the two, a small night stand.

On the opposite side of the room, I found a desk with a plug for my computer and a tall thin window that looked out across the gentle sweep of the hill down onto the ocean. No mirrors, no magazines, no frills, just the necessities.

I slipped off my flip-flops and felt immediately a gentle heat pulsing up through the floor. "Heated floors!" I thought. "Very nice, brothers!" Nothing about this room was wasted. It was bare and essential, but also utterly comfortable. I opened my laptop, plugged it in, arranged my toiletries, and then sunk down onto the bed, suddenly aware that I had nothing to do. No dinner to make. No daughter to entertain. No laundry to switch over. No papers to grade. My time was inexplicably my own, and I spun for a moment in the space of such freedom.

I found on the bedside table a welcome card listing the prayer times and meal times of the abbey. I could, if I wished, get up at 4 a.m. to pray with the brothers, but there were other prayer times too, again at 7 a.m., then at 10, and 3, and so on.

My plan for the weekend had been to do nothing but write and read, but I decided to add prayer to the agenda. I would attend the evening chant before dinner and join the brothers again the following day as much as I could.

Suddenly, there was a knock at the door. I opened it to find another brother, his skin as pale and translucent as vellum, his eyes bloodshot. He smiled kindly, but would not hold my gaze, instead choosing to look somewhere toward my feet."

"Are you comfortable?" he asked.

"Yes, this is lovely,"

"I've brought your towels." He handed me a stack of neatly folded towels, still warm from the drier. "And if you need to adjust the heat, the dial is right inside by the bed." He pointed into the room, bending awkwardly over the threshold trying to signal around the corner. I stepped quickly out of his way, expecting him to come in and show me. But he didn't. He stood rooted to his spot.

"Oh, of course," I thought. "He probably won't enter a room alone with a woman."

"Dinner will be served in half an hour," he said, then left.

I decided that thirty minutes wasn't enough time to do any sort of writing, so I slipped my flip-flops back on and headed out to the western grounds around the abbey, to a prayer labyrinth.

After two years of scrambling for any spare moment for myself, this weekend felt like an unequivocal luxury.

"This place is awesome!" I texted Dwayne. "There's a silent dining room. A prayer labyrinth. I can go pray with the brothers. I don't have to talk to anyone for over 78 hours!"

"Sounds awful," he texted back. I chuckled. Of course my extroverted husband would find a weekend away in silence, flanked by quiet monks, close to torture. I snapped the phone shut and sunk quietly into the prayer labyrinth and my weekend of writing and contemplation.

St. Benedict instructed his disciples to be humble in their hospitality. He wrote, "All humility should be shown in addressing a guest on arrival or departure." He also instructed the brothers that "every kindness is shown to [the guest]. . . . The superior may break his fast for the sake of the guest. . . . The abbot shall pour water on the hands of the guests, and the abbot with the entire community shall wash their feet."[1]

Thank goodness no one at the abbey tried to wash my feet, but I did find in their presence the same mixture of humility and hospitality that St. Benedict laid out in his rules for the order. As the years have slid by, and as I've begun to learn more about the art of being good company, I've often thought that this same mixture of humility and hospitality undergirds the experience of good company too.

Good learning partners (as Marcia Baxter Magolda calls those who walk with us in our twenties) are always balancing opposing goals: They are challenging and supporting us, and they are both pushing us to be autonomous, while also pushing us to connect with others in meaningful ways.

See the dilemma here? If good company has any ounce of self-importance, any whisper of dominance, anything and everything we are trying to accomplish on our journey to discover who God has created us to be is immediately negated. The point after all is not for us to learn to listen to another wise voice outside of ourselves. The entire heart and soul and center of finding our place in this world is for us to learn how to know ourselves in the midst of all these voices, and build an internal foundation upon which we can build the rest of our lives.

So, good company is built on the principle of humility. A good learning partner recognizes his or her place in our journey, not in front of us, or even beside us, but behind us, spurring us on when we want to give up, but catching us when we start to fall.

By so doing, good company is also enacting a profound ritual of hospitality. As Margaret Guenther, an Episcopal priest and spiritual director, writes so profoundly, "Hospitality offers more than comfort: it also ensures physical survival. Spiritually, too, we cannot make it through the desert or across the frontier alone."[2] The truth is, so often our journey through our twenties can feel like a pilgrimage through the desert, one where the compass has been ripped from our hands. There is so much to traverse in our young adult years—leaving behind home; discovering a sense of ourselves and a sense of place; and deciding what career we want to settle on, which partner to marry, what faith we will cling to or let go, which political party to embrace.

Good company is hospitality because not only do they offer us comfort as we are trying to piece together meaning and identity, but they also help us survive the miles and years of terrain we have to journey to get there. This is perhaps the single best bit of news in all of the upheaval of our twenties. Yes, there is a good chance we will fall apart. Yes, there will be pain and panic and grief, but *no* we do not have to go it alone. We do not have to make sense of it all by ourselves.

It is precisely at the juncture of our darkest moments, when we are most confused and jumbled, that good company slides in behind us, puts a hand on our backs and says, "Go on. Keep moving. Don't stop here." In this way, good company touches our journey with both the humility to take the back seat, and the hospitality to offer us companionship in the wilderness.

3
ROLL THE BOAT

The first few days in Bellingham were a slow creep out from center, as we gradually unpacked and began to explore our new home. I discovered gorgeous parks in our new leafy green home, one of which was Boulevard Park, the darling of Bellingham. Situated on the shoulder of the bay, right next to the water, everyone loved to go to Boulevard on summer days. As Noelle scrambled over the large ship fashioned with toys, loops, and slides for the kids, I noted my surroundings. The water of Northern Puget Sound, which licked the shoulder of the park, was calm and easy. Small waves dimpled the surface, winking at the gray sky. On the horizon, a haze of islands whispered back across the surface of the water. These were the San Juan Islands, an archipelago of over four hundred islands located just off the bay of Bellingham. In those crystal blue waters, orcas play and sea kayakers bob along the surface.

It wasn't long before we found ourselves out on that water. Dwayne, Noelle, and I soon learned how to canoe together, Dwayne pulling hard on the paddles to cut through waves. Noelle dipping her three-year-old arms into the water up to her elbows. Me balancing a picnic on my knees.

Because of that beautiful water crested by hills and islands, we met and befriended Dong.

Western had a sailing team, and Dong was an avid sailer. He took Dwayne out on the bay and taught him how to maneuver a small sailboat, no bigger than the size of a dining room table. Dong stood at the helm in his khaki shorts and flip-flops, calling instructions to Dwayne as they both pulled ropes and leaned into the wind.

"I'm going to teach you how to roll the boat," Dong announced one day as they marched out onto the dock for another day of sailing. Because these boats were small, when the wind was rough and the conditions just right, it wasn't uncommon for them to flip over, plunging bodies beneath the icy water. When that happens, it's possible to flip the boat upright again, and Dong wanted to teach Dwayne how to do this.

Dwayne's eyes bulged at Dong's announcement, but he strapped on his life vest and dutifully followed Dong out to the dock.

As we spent more time with Dong, I came to learn the remarkable details of his story, not just out of college, but during college.

"Dong is a Vietnamese name," he explained to me once. In Vietnam, his name is pronounced something like "Dowm," but the pronunciation has gotten lost in translation. Dong understood from an early age that his family was different from the families around him, and along with that came deep expectations from his parents that would determine the path of his future. It had always been important to them that Dong choose a career that would provide for him and create security; and in their mind, security was synonymous with money.

As a child, Dong wanted to be an astronaut. When he told his father this, his dad shook his head in dismay. "You don't want to be an astronaut," he said. "It's dangerous, and you could die."

"OK, well, fair enough," Dong thought. He took this in stride. A little later on in school, Dong decided that he wanted to be an artist. When this new aspiration came up in conversation, he found the same look of dismay painted across his father's face. "You can't be an artist because they don't make any money!" "OK, well, fine," Dong thought, and went on his way.

Finally, in middle school Dong stumbled across a career he thought he might love. "I had an amazing history teacher," Dong explained to me once. "He was incredible. Everything that came out of his mouth . . . I had to listen. He was funny and engaging. I wanted to be a teacher."

One evening, Dong overheard his mother and father talking about his cousin who lived in Washington, D.C., and had started his career as a high school teacher.

"He's so stupid!" Dong's mother complained. "He's throwing his life away." Her words beat the air like a hammer, pounding into Dong's heart one very strong conviction—he would never tell his mother and father of his dreams to teach, because they would surely think he was a failure. While he chose to keep his aspirations secret from his family, they didn't die. His curiosity about teaching only strengthened in high school, where he met and learned under more inspiring teachers.

Until this point in his life, the external voices of Dong's parents worked like paring knives, cutting away what they believed to be the unnecessary fat of his future. After high school, Dong knew his parents would pay his way through college, but this generous gift came with some major conditions: (1) They expected him to attend University of Washington just a few blocks away from their house in Seattle; (2) they expected him to live in their basement to save money; and (3) they expected him to study accounting, because this was a no-nonsense career in which he could make lots of money.

None of these expectations sounded appealing to Dong. In fact, he was so distraught by his parents' dream for his life that he had nearly zero motivation to apply for college. But a combination of peer pressure and a feeling of being unprepared for the workforce ultimately tipped Dong over the edge and he began sending out college applications. He applied not only to University of Washington, but another school that caught his attention, Western Washington University in the rainy, leafy, vibrant little city of Bellingham. Much to his relief, he was declined from UW, and accepted to Western.

To make up to his parents for the fact that he wasn't going to their dream school, nor live in their basement, he acquiesced and chose accounting as a major. "I did it so my parents would be happy," he told me. "And they were happy. But I wasn't."

You would have thought that this would have been the end of the matter for Dong. That his parents would have relinquished their expectations for him and his future and let him finally sail off onto the waters of independence with their blessing. But it wasn't, and they didn't.

Dong's dad made him promise to apply to University of Washington every quarter until he was able to get in. The first year of college, Dong didn't really put up a fight with his father about this. He was unhappy in his major at Western, and he also was struggling to connect and make friends. He went home nearly every weekend that first year.

But then, at the end of his freshman year, something remarkable happened. He got a letter saying that someone had nominated him to be an RA, residents' advisor. As he researched just what the RAs did, he read things like, "Serve as a peer advisor and educator to approximately fifty residential hall students," and "implement lesson plans as a part of the Residential Education Model." This job description sounded like a fantastic way to connect to the community, but also more importantly, it contained echoes of a job which Dong had always dreamed of, but never allowed himself to pursue. "Peer educator" and "lesson plans" sounded an awful lot like teaching at some level.

Dong threw himself into the application process and waited with baited breath to see if he was hired. He wasn't that first year, but he was undeterred. He knew he would try again his sophomore year.

By the middle of his sophomore year, college was beginning to shape up into a much different experience for Dong. He still didn't enjoy his major, but by this point, he had started to make some meaningful connections with friends, and these friends had begun to paint a picture of the world for Dong that he had never considered before. They made him feel as if who he was outweighed any amount of success his career or job afforded.

Dong relayed his story to me: "I was accepted now by my friends because of who I was, not what I was studying. I was starting to fit in more at Western than when I was home." Suddenly, he didn't feel a need to go home every weekend, and when he did, he realized that he almost felt more comfortable, more seen, more known at school than he did with his own family.

Scholar of adult education, Dr. Laurent Daloz might describe Dong's separation from home as a primary task facing all of us in our twenties. He would say it's the main thing we have to do. We have to reframe the world we once knew in a radically new way. He wrote, "This does not mean that the old world has been abandoned; rather, it has been incorporated into a broader awareness of its place. It is *seen* in a new way."[1] This is precisely what was happening to Dong. He was beginning to see his mom and dad, their values, and his family in the broader context of his friends' and professors' worldviews. To his schoolmates and professors, it didn't matter if he was an accounting major or not. He had value in simply being himself.

But simply because he saw his home and parents with new eyes didn't mean that they held any less sway over his life. He still loved his family, and they loved him. It was midway through his sophomore year that his dad sat him down.

"Apply to University of Washington just one more time and I'll drop it." A wave of excitement broke over Dong. He had been applying every quarter for a year and a half. Suddenly, he saw a light at the end of the tunnel.

He immediately called a friend. "This is it!" he said giddily into the receiver. "Do you want to help me write the worst application ever?"

Together Dong and his friend set out to write a terrible entrance essay. The cursor blinked on a blank page. "I am an Asian bonsai tree," Dong wrote.

"That's good!" his friend slapped him on the back. "Add, 'My roots go deep.'"

Dong chuckled and typed the words. He was purposefully mocking his ethnicity and heritage and in so doing, he believed there was no way he was going to get accepted to such a competitive school.

The next day Dong mailed the application and forgot about UW completely. He turned his attention to applying again for the resident advisor position, spending his evenings chatting with his friends who were already resident advisors.

A few weeks later, his phone rang. He reached into pocket and saw his mother's name marching across the screen in black lines.

"Pack your bags," she announced. "You've been accepted to UW. You're leaving tomorrow."

Suddenly, the boat of Dong's life flipped and plunged him beneath the water. He hung up with his mother and stumbled back to his room. He had exactly one afternoon to figure out just how to tell his mom and dad no.

He had never expected this. He had hoped that the decision would be made for him and that the difficult conversation would never have to happen, but here he was suddenly forced to stand up to his parents and make clear to them what he had felt all along. He could taste salt in the back of his throat. His appetite had completely evaporated.

That evening, as he sat in the quiet of his room, he watched as his fingers pushed the buttons of his phone. He was unsure of what he was going to say, how he was going to say it, and how his parents would react.

"Hello," he heard the familiar voice of his dad over the phone.

Suddenly, Dong was talking, though he did not know what he said. He didn't even register what he was saying until he reached this sentence: "No, I'm not going to go to University of Washington."

The line went deathly silent and Dong felt a chill up his spine. "Mom? Dad?"

Suddenly a blur of fury broke on the other end of the call. Voices shouting, arguing at him from miles away and yet so close, so hot on his ears. "Fine!" his father retorted. "You stay at Western, but we're not paying and . . . and you can never come home."

The voices went dead. They hung up.

With the rush of that single sentence, the floor cracked and shattered beneath Dong's feet. He sunk beneath the waters. Everything he had stood on to get to that point was ripped away from him. He was suddenly completely out on his own with no sense of direction.

"I had no idea how much college cost, or what it took to stay in college. I went to academic advising, and said, 'What are loans?' I applied to several jobs. I didn't get any jobs. It was very scary because I didn't know. I was questioning whether I was making the right choice."

The only thing that kept Dong going forward was that every time he replayed the conversation in his mind, he kept making the same choice. He knew there was nothing else he would have done in that moment. So, spared from regret, he was able to focus on the task at hand: staying in college.

Yet he was also conflicted with a deeper battle. For the first time, he had to step back and reckon with all his motivations. Why was he in college? Why was he choosing to stay at Western? Why had he chosen this institution, this network of strangers, over his own family?

The week after his painful conversation with his parents, Dong found out that he had been picked as a resident advisor for the following year and that it would include his room and board. That was a huge opportunity. Now he only had to worry about paying for tuition.

In that vulnerable state, stripped of the support and shelter of family, thrust out into the chill of the world, Dong stumbled onto a realization. He was talking to a friend when it suddenly occurred to him that he didn't have to do accounting anymore.

He leapt out off his bed and dashed out into the hall, suddenly overcome with excitement. "I'm going to be a teacher!" he crooned.

Finally, Dong was free to make his own choice. It was as if suddenly the lens to his future clicked into place and he saw himself in bright and rosy detail. For the first time, he was going to be able to do what he had always dreamed of.

But then something both remarkable and strange happened.

Dong's father called back a week after their big fight in which he had disowned his son.

"Son?" a cracked voice reached him.

"Yeah, I can hear you, Dad." Dong listened as his father spoke in a brittle voice, riddled with tears.

"I'm so sorry." Dong had never heard his father cry before. "If you want to stay at Western, that's OK with us."

At that moment, Dong found himself at another crossroads. It felt like a miracle that his father was apologizing to him, and he did not want to treat such a gesture lightly. He saw three options opening up before him. First, he could accept his father's apology and then deliver another heart-breaking piece of news: "I want to be a teacher too." He knew this would shake his parents to their core. He knew how they felt about his cousin who had pursued the same career, and he was certain it would cause them just as much pain and anxiety as his proclamation that he did not want to return home to study at the big state school down the street.

His second option was to choose to walk away from his father's money and try to work and study at the same time and pursue his dream of teaching. This thought overwhelmed him. Even though he had been hired as an RA, that job didn't cover tuition and he was unsure how to find another job on top of the twenty hours a week required of him by the residence life department. He also knew that this option still brought the very real risk of losing his parents' blessing over his career.

The final option was to accept his father's apology and money and go back to studying accounting and be satisfied with the victory he had just won in being able to stay at the school he chose rather than the school his parents chose for him.

It was a tough decision, and who of us in our early twenties would be able to make it? In the end, Dong chose option number three. He accepted his father's apology and his money and decided to continue with accounting even though he loathed the subject.

Dong started his junior year as a resident advisor, and sunk quickly into his new responsibilities. He not only planned regular community events that helped his fifty-plus students mingle, but he also conducted four one-on-one conversations a year, wherein he asked them meaningful questions designed to make them reflect on their own identity development: "How are you different now from when you were in high school? What's been the hardest part of this year for you?"

Meanwhile, in his new role, Dong was discovering a whole new passion he'd never known before. "When I became an RA . . . that changed my life," he told me. "It introduced a whole new me. Now I had a support system reflecting, 'Why are you here? Why are you doing this?' That changed me. That was when I was able to think more about why I was doing the things I was doing."

As you can imagine, Dong had a tangle of motivations and actions to work through in his own life. First of which was trying to figure out the pressure he felt from his family on every side to be successful. Second, his own unwavering commitment to a major in accounting, which he knew he despised. And then finally, an underlying discomfort he felt with his identity as a Vietnamese-American. These were all issues that had roiled and tangled beneath the surface of Dong's life that contributed to decisions he didn't quite understand.

Thankfully, while Dong was asking his residents the kind of questions that forced them to reflect on their identity, he was getting the same sort of challenge and support from his supervisor, the resident director, Anton.

"So tell me," Anton asked Dong one afternoon in his office, "are you ready for some tough questions today?"

Dong's brow creased, but he nodded, dutifully marching into the conversation.

"As we've been talking this year, in our one-on-ones, you've made it really clear you don't like your major. So, why are you studying accounting?"

Dong's mouth suddenly went dry, and his tongue caught on the back of his mouth. "Because it's successful in my mind," Dong offered.

Anton frowned. "Why do you want to be successful?"

Dong and Anton went back and forth like this for an hour, with Dong offering every answer he had heard his parents rehearse and Anton gently pushing him to unravel his own motivations further and further. By the end of the meeting, Dong's eyes were wet with tears. With the persistent challenge of Anton's questions, Dong began to see that all his parents wanted was for him to be happy, but that was easier wished than done. It wasn't as if Dong could go to his parents and tell them, "Hey, Mom, Dad, being a teacher is going to make me happier." For him, for his family, it didn't work that way.

Having this sort of realization through Anton's questions liberated Dong. It didn't lead him to change his major, though he knew it was a career choice he would not enjoy. It did, however, help him to see clearly why he was making the decisions he was making. It helped him see for the first time what was motivating his parents, and allowed him to sit in the untidiness of life and find a way forward for himself. Even if he continued in a major he didn't enjoy, it was at least a decision he could finally make for himself, not for his parents.

In his book *Self and Society*, Nevitt Sanford introduces the idea of challenge and support as instrumental tools in helping us develop our identity.[2] The basic idea is that none of us will grow unless we're pushed out of ourselves and forced to innovate and generate new responses to the world around us; hence the need for challenge. But at the same time, often the challenge and the new circumstance can be very stressful. If we're not careful, we'll inadvertently revert back to the shell of our adolescence, becoming hardened versions of our younger selves. For this reason, we also need support so we don't get overwhelmed.

Just as good company must learn to balance humility and hospitality, he or she must also learn to balance challenge and support—two seemingly oppositional forces. As Dong's supervisor and friend, Anton had a unique position to walk. He needed to roll Dong's boat, but then also help him learn how to flip it upright again.

By asking these tough questions and also encouraging Dong as he wrestled with the answers, Anton was doing three things. First, he was helping Dong deal with the complex issues tangling up both his personal and work life. Second, Anton was pushing Dong to develop his own personal authority. Finally, Anton's probing questions were allowing Dong an opportunity to work collaboratively with Anton to solve the problem of his conflicted feelings about his major and his relationship with his parents.

Ultimately, Anton used his resources and experiences in residence life to encourage Dong to study student affairs after graduation. Dong was an extraordinary resident advisor and showed much potential for working with students in higher education. And that's exactly what he's doing right now. Three years after graduation, Dong is applying for graduate programs in College Counseling and Student Affairs. He'll probably never be a teacher in the traditional sense, but he recognizes in this career an opportunity to bring together so many of his interests and natural strengths.

He told me, "It was a defining moment, being an RA. I got some of the leadership and mentorship that I enjoyed. I think I got more out of the experience of being an RA than my residents because I grew and changed a lot."

Anton's good company, along with the good company of his fellow resident advisors saved Dong from settling into a splintered sense of self. Their challenge and support helped him find a way forward and a vocation that finally fit him. He learned to sail on the seas of his sense of self.

Dwayne came back from his day of sailing with Dong, soaking wet.

"How did it go?" I asked, amused.

"Cold and wet." Dwayne smiled. I imagined the two of them out on the water, the small white boat tipping its axis and rolling with gravity. I imagined Dwayne and Dong popping up beside the boat, their arms reaching and pulling to flip it upright again.

"Did it work?" I pressed. "Did you get the boat out of the water."

"Yeah!" Dwayne nodded. "Dong is a good teacher."

4

FOLDING OUT FROM CENTER

I walked across campus, the white sidewalk cutting a pretty curve over the lawn of green. To my left, Old Main stood regal and aged, its brick face as weathered and stately as any Ivy League school I had visited on the East Coast. Old Main was the oldest building on campus, in fact, the original building on campus. One hundred years earlier, Western had been a teaching college for women, and Old Main had been the whole college, housing both the dormitory rooms and the classrooms.

Now, a century later, I was walking across the lawn to the center of a campus that had unfolded like petals from this original building. All around me stately brick buildings with ivy crawling up crevices guarded over the sacred ground of learning. I was making my way to one such building, only this one was flanked by a rose garden rather than ivy. I carried my own curriculum vitae in hopes that the head of the English department would look kindly on me and give me a teaching job in the writing department. I had taught freshman composition for four years in L.A., had completed my master of fine arts from Antioch University of Los Angeles, and was certainly qualified to teach part time, or what we call "adjunct" in the higher education world. But I had also learned during my time in L.A. that one needs to hustle to get adjunct positions. You have to make connections, meet the right people, and show up at the right time in order to get a job. It's not as simple as filling out an application and waiting for an interview.

Most of the time, prospective adjuncts are placed in a pool where we jostle around, waiting to be seen and picked when a course becomes available. And if we are lucky enough to get pulled from the dregs of the pool and placed into a classroom with students and real-life curriculum, then our contracts run semester by semester, and so, for the first year or so, we are living without any guarantee that we'll have a job the following semester.

"Just take a seat. He'll be right with you," the secretary of the English department said pleasantly. I walked back out into the corridor to find a seat. A few moments later, the head of the department opened his door and signaled me in.

"Hi! Come in!" He was a handsome older man with salt-and-pepper hair and an easy air about him. "Tell me about yourself," he said.

I sat in the chair across from his desk. Around me shelves of books touched the ceiling, and papers and file folders burst from their holdings along his desk and coffee table. I introduced myself and explained that we had just moved from Los Angeles where I had taught at three different universities for four years. I also told him that I happened to live on campus since my husband worked in the residence life department. He smiled blankly and nodded.

"So I live right across the lawn," I said, signaling out his window in the direction of Edens Hall. I'm not sure why I felt it necessary to drive this point home. Perhaps I thought proximity would bolster my chances of getting a class. But it didn't.

He thanked me, shook my hand, and told me to send in all my application materials. Which I did. A few months later, well into the school year, I received a note saying I had been added to the adjunct pool and would be contacted if any classes became available.

"If you don't know someone over in that department, you're never going to see the light of day," a new friend told me. She was right. I never did see the light of day, though I tried to make contact with others in the department. I also applied to the local community college, the technical college, and the community college in the next county over, but still nothing gave, nothing shifted, and teaching continued to elude me.

For the first time since becoming a mother, I was a stay-at-home mom.

"How do you do this? What is your routine?" my fingers clicked away at the keyboard as I sent out a plea to all my friends who were also stay-at-home moms.

I pushed away from the keyboard and looked at Noelle, then at the clock. Nine o'clock in the morning. "Do you want to go to the park?" I asked.

Noelle jumped up and down on the couch, her body careening first into the painting on the wall and then the lamp shades on the end tables. Outside a delicate mist of rain coated everything in beads. "We could go to the library," I offered. "Or we could go grocery shopping, or we could stay here, or we could . . ." Noelle hit the lamp and it came crashing to the ground. I sat listless.

Everything and nothing needed to be done. Everything and nothing was important. There was no schedule to my days without work, no driving to-do list, no larger structure to my weeks and months. I felt as if I had crashed squarely into an existential crisis.

I got up and walked back to the bedroom, leaving Noelle and the lamp behind. A fist squeezed my chest in a steady and firm grip. I sunk down on to the bed and let the tears flow. "Why am I crying?" I asked myself. "What's going on?" I waited; I listened; and I let myself go. Little by little, as I felt myself grieve, I realized I missed work, that even though I had only ever taught part-time, a part of my identity had been wrapped up in teaching.

I pushed myself off the bed and marched back out to the living room. Noelle had her head in the refrigerator and was pulling milk and eggs off the shelves and onto the floor.

"Come on," I said. "Let's go to the library."

Little by little, I began to discover a daily and weekly routine that worked for Noelle and me. I discovered which part of the day worked best to go out and explore, and which part of the day was best for staying home and resting. Through the help of my mom friends back in L.A., I also learned how to turn my home into a playschool for Noelle full of crafts and science experiments. We made homemade play dough and turned our kitchen into a kid-sized bakery. And we burned through boxes and boxes of baking soda watching it magically explode when mixed with vinegar and water. In gradual shifts, I was learning how to organize my life around this new center—a two-bedroom apartment on the second floor of a residence hall. And while I was discovering new petals of joy in being at home with Noelle, I also grieved the loss, not just of my teaching, but also my writing.

I had actually been working on a book ever since my first days of pregnancy with Noelle, and with much toil and discipline I had arrived at a first draft of the book by her third birthday.

Over the summer, right before we moved to Bellingham, we took a three-week jaunt to Marion, Indiana, to visit my parents. While there, I had contacted my writing professor from Indiana Wesleyan University, Dr. Mary Brown. It had been in Dr. Brown's writing courses that my first attraction to writing sparked, and it had been under her careful and demanding guidance that I found myself reduced to tears more than once. Frankly, Dr. Brown demanded more of me than I often thought I could achieve, and yet she managed to get my best work out of me. It was she who taught me how to be disciplined in writing. And it was she who introduced me to some of the finest writing I've read in my entire life, great authors and poets who to this day live in my head and heart.

I asked Dr. Brown if she would be willing to read the first draft of my book, and to my amazement, she agreed. I printed off a copy at the local printshop, had it bound and mailed it to her. By the time I arrived in Marion for vacation, she had read the draft.

"Could we talk about it in person?" she e-mailed me.

"Certainly!" I responded. "Would you like to meet for coffee?"

That summer I pulled up to the Gaither Resource Center, a cute little Christian bookstore and café situated on a long stretch of country road in central Indiana. Inside, the store was perfumed with the aroma of coffee and scented candles. To the left, merchandise poured from every shelf and display stand, cramming the little space with more ideas than it had room to rightly hold. Cookbooks and specialty foods gave way to a kids' corner with stuffed animals any grandmother would be hard-pressed not to squeeze and buy on the spot. Beyond the kids' corner were more shelves filled with books and specialty items for Christian living: clothing, jewelry, CDs, and DVDs. The café took up the right side of the store, and I pushed my way past all the merchandise, scanning the faces to see if I could find Dr. Brown.

She sat beside a window, her phone in her hands, as she lightly touched the screen, scanning e-mails. She looked up at me and broke into a wide grin, spreading her arms for a hug.

As we sat at the table sipping our respective drinks, she took out my manuscript with its shiny black binding and placed it carefully between us. She pressed her lips together for a moment of thought and then said, "Your sweet spirit shines through, but it has a lot of weaknesses."

I dropped my chin and looked at the manuscript. She still had her hand on it, as if she were holding my heart, patting it gently.

She went over her critiques, and as she spoke, her words resonated. I knew she was right.

Behind us the espresso machine squealed. "The voice isn't quite right," she said. "It seems too young for you. I want to hear more of your reflections on what was happening, not just the descriptions." I nodded. The circle of classy grandmothers beside us paid their bill, dotted their mouths with their napkins, and got up to look at the clothing in the back of the store. "And I think the chronology is wrong somehow too," Dr. Brown continued. "I think you should just tell the story from the beginning."

We finished our drinks and gave each other one last hug.

"Thank you so much," I said.

She held my shoulders for a moment and looked me in the eyes, "What you're doing is important, and I'm so proud of you."

I nodded and felt my eyes prick with tears. I went back to my parents' house certain of two things: first, I would be Dr. Brown's fan for the rest of my days; and second, I needed to rewrite my book.

So when I returned to Bellingham, at the end of July, I came ready to teach and ready to write. But with teaching evaporating from my future, so did my source of income to pay for childcare and time to write.

"I don't know how I'm going to do it!" I complained to my friend Kristin over the phone. "How am I supposed to finish this book with only nap times and bedtimes to write?" I was in a foul mood, pouting all over myself.

My friend's voice grew firm on the other end of the line. I could imagine the dimple in her smooth cheek punctuating each word and her light eyes looking right into my face: "The time you have to write is the time you have, Christin. And you'll be a better writer for it!"

I snapped up as if I'd been swiftly kicked in the behind. Kristin's message was clear. No more moping! It was time to dig in and work.

She had just written and published her first book and if anyone knew the psychological battle and sheer cliff face of effort it takes to complete a major work of prose, it was Kristin. She was not going to let me sink into the quicksand of self-pity.

I sat stunned into silence, measuring Kristin's words and my circumstances. I had left everything behind in L.A.—my teaching, my friends, my support network, my writing. But two things remained—my family and my creativity. There was much to let go of and much to grieve, but Kristin's challenge reminded me that I had no excuses when it came to building the kind of life I wanted to live, and being the kind of wife, mother, and professional I was capable of being.

After that evening, I slowly began to unfurl, pushing out into a new rhythm, a new vision for my days and my identity. I wouldn't say that the flower of my life bloomed just then, because there were still dark days and challenges ahead, but through the challenge and support of both Dr. Brown and Kristin, the bud of a future stood curled inside of me waiting to unfold.

5

COEXIST

I stood outside Emily's door skimming the signs and pictures decorating the smooth wood surface. One sticker in particular caught my attention: "Coexist." Religious symbols replaced the letters—the crescent of Islam, the star of David, the cross of Christianity. Our apartment was across the hallway, and I waited beneath the fluorescent lights of the corridor for Emily to answer.

Earlier that day, Dwayne stopped by the apartment. "Emily's sick. Could you bring her some tea or something?"

"Sure!" I chirped, and went to my cupboards to see what I could find. I was eager to meet another one of Dwayne's RAs, and to play my new role as "dorm mom."

Emily opened the door, a rumpled mess. Her hair hung in limp strands around her puffy face. If she wore spacers in her earlobes, they were gone at that moment and only the empty holes remained. She smiled weakly, and I noticed two cute dimples. Whatever coolness emanated from her, the sickness had seriously muffled it.

"Hi," I spoke quickly, suddenly feeling self-conscious about disturbing her. "I'm Dwayne's wife. He told me you weren't feeling well, and I wanted to bring you this." I handed her the cup of tea. "If you need anything else, just let me know. I'll be happy to share our dinner with you so you don't have to go over to the cafeteria."

"Thanks," she said and her eyes lit with a burst of gratitude. "This is so nice of you!" She reached out and I noted an elegant tattoo around her forearm—a single line circling her arm and centered by a tiny coffee mug.

I didn't get to talk much to Emily that day, but it didn't take long for me to discover just what made her so special. She was indeed a cool girl: quiet, thoughtful, direct, and hip. Nothing about her was expected, from her style, to her interests, to her way of thinking. She often saw things in a unique way and asked questions that hadn't occurred to me.

I remember asking her one day about the "Coexist" sticker on her door. If I'm honest, I knew I would like her from the moment

I saw that sticker. I appreciate the gentle spirit behind a sticker that would call for understanding and acceptance. To me, that sticker revealed a young woman aware of a spiritual reality, and a heart longing for tolerance in the face of oppression, violence, and war.

"I was raised in a Christian home," she told me. "I grew up going to Sunday school and church camp and all that, but I think a breaking point came for me about halfway through Anthropology 101." Her class was covering world religions and had started to move away from the major belief systems of Catholicism, Protestantism, Hinduism, Buddhism, and Islam. At that point, Emily's professor turned the class's attention toward the smaller, localized creation stories around the world, particularly in the non-Western world.

"The viewfinder in my head zoomed out faster than I could handle," Emily explained, her voice growing quiet. "It put me into a tailspin of trying to grasp the number of varying perspectives in the world. I suddenly felt pretty ridiculous for thinking that I had any idea what was really going on—not just in the realm of belief systems, but in every aspect of what it means to be a person."

I could appreciate just how earth-shaking it would be for a nineteen-year-old to suddenly learn that Christianity was not the only belief system in the world, and instead that a multitude of belief systems texture our creation. Emily chuckled, "All of this was before I even knew what 'existential crisis' meant."

I laughed. Yes, that sounded very much like an existential crisis to me. Even as I laughed, I couldn't help but think of the first of Marcia Baxter Magolda's six principles for good company. She says that learning partners help us learn that knowledge is both complex and socially constructed.[1] The moment that Emily's professor introduced her to all those other creation stories, she pushed Emily to come face-to-face with the fact that everything she knew about religion was not as simple as she once thought and was in fact shaped by those around her.

Dr. John Purdie, the associate director of the resident life program at Western, says that the idea that knowledge is socially constructed comes from a theory called social constructivism. This theory starts with the premise that "we didn't dig in a cave one day and find a box and inside was geometry or history or anything else," Dr. Purdie explained. "All knowledge is a social construction. We call dad, 'Dad,' because we've all agreed that's what we call him."[2] In other words, we know what we know because those who have gone before us have all agreed upon the foundations of our understanding, and these foundations are being shaped every day in an active way.

So when Emily took Anthropology 101 and learned about the many different creation myths around the world, she had a rather brutal encounter with social constructivism. These tribes around the world had all agreed upon their own creation myths, and as a result of this understanding, Emily called into question her own experience with Christianity.

If I could be so presumptuous as to put words to her thought process during that period, it might sound something like this: "Wait, so if they can just create their own stories about the beginning of the world and God and faith, how do I know that Christianity is not also a simple creation of society? How do I know faith in all its grandeur is not also man-made?"

Is it any wonder that she threw her hands up in the air and walked away from faith altogether? She felt completely overwhelmed by this new perspective.

So if being good company means that we make people question the very fabric of their beliefs, causing them to maybe even walk away from those convictions altogether, how on earth is being good company a good thing? How is having good company valuable for our growth as individuals learning to live in a complex and difficult world?

Well, that's my point exactly. We live in a complex and nuanced world, a world in which a simple, black-and-white understanding of ourselves and life cannot stand the test of time. If we never face the reality that everything we know has been touched in one way or another by flesh-and-blood people, if we never come to terms with the fact that the world is full of other legitimate experiences different from our own, then we run the risk of shattering on the hard edges of life. Or at the very best, we risk growing into our silver years as a stunted version of our younger selves.

The truth is, we understand God and faith through man. That God-man's name was Jesus. Just because our faith is socially constructed, shaped by flesh-and-blood apostles, doesn't mean that it is somehow invalid. Just because others may live different lifestyles from our own, does not mean that our lifestyle is somehow wrong. And just because others may arrive at different conclusions about problems than we do, does not mean that our conclusions are baseless.

Here is the leap we must make as young adults; here is the leap we must help our friends make as we seek to be good company: We must come to the place where we can say, "I know there are multiple perspectives in the world, but those perspectives do not impinge upon my sense of right and wrong."[3]

As Dr. Purdie put it, "Here's my criteria that I own. I am right, and here's why I am right. I recognize others have [different] criteria, and I recognize other perspectives, and that's OK, but that doesn't mean I'm wrong."[4] What Dr. Purdie illustrates here is that once we are able, as young adults, to recognize that knowledge is socially constructed, we are able to move into a place of knowing that reaches beyond the rigid delineations of yes and no, this and that, us and them. We see the world as a glorious array of thoughts, ideas, experiences, and realities. We become supple in our thought, vital in our ability to navigate these myriad vistas, and certain of our ability to identify truth.

One truth does exist among the many, and good company knows that we will never fully embrace this truth as our own until we are forced to reckon with our ability to arrive at knowing and knowledge. We must become meta-thinkers. We must be able not only to think, but to step outside ourselves and understand why we think the way we think and how we've arrived at our understanding.

In this way, we are not left with merely coexisting in the world with so many other experiences and realities, as the sticker on Emily's door imagines. Instead, we can go a step beyond that. We are able to see, experience, acknowledge, even empathize with those around us and their experience of life. But ultimately, we learn to integrate the many elements of this life into a single and redemptive whole.

6

MULTIPLICITY AND RELATIVISM

Part of integrating the many perspectives we discover in the world into a single, redemptive whole is learning how to build on the recognition that knowledge is socially constructed and formulate our own sense of conviction. In other words, we find our due north and stick to it. How do we do this when there are so many experiences of the world, of truth, of God?

All too often, I think we as young adults feel like the only options we have are to either fall into fundamentalism or multiplicity. We feel we need to rigidly and literally hold on to the principles handed to us from our pasts. We feel we must be defined by intolerance and opposition. But if this approach to people, relationships, and ideas makes us more than a little uncomfortable, then we feel the only other option is multiplicity. The idea that everybody is right, everything is right, and all paths lead to truth. Dr. John Purdie describes multiplicity this way: "Someone in the throes of multiplicity would say that Hitler was right for Hitler. They might say, 'Now he wasn't right for me, although lots of people agreed with him then, but Hitler was right for Hitler.'"[1] In other words, there are no absolutes to build our beliefs on, except, of course, for the absolute of tolerance.

As we can see, there are many potential problems with multiplicity, not the least of which is that it gives us no firm foundation on which to build our own identity, conviction, or future. Multiplicity leads us into a kind of splintered knowing, one that denies what I believe is the very basic, God-given need for meaning-making. How can we build an interpretation of the world, ourselves, and God when everything is right and therefore nothing is right?

Part of our journey as young adults is finding good company that will help us avoid the shadowlands of multiplicity and help us discover our credence, a foundation upon which to build our future and make decisions.

It's been fascinating for me to watch our friends in their early twenties wrestling with multiplicity and their own convictions. One such friend is Molly, one of Dwayne's RAs at Western.

Molly is tall, fair as a Tolkien elf, with cheeks that both smile and blush easily. Molly and her boyfriend were a sweet couple, so I was shocked when at the end of the year, Molly came to our apartment with tears in her eyes. I fixed her tea, and we sat on the couch in the quiet of the evening. Noelle lay asleep in the other room.

"So what's on your mind?" I asked. I could see the tears pricking her eyes.

"Well, I'm just trying to figure out some relationship stuff." I nodded and waited for her to go on. "You see, I started going to church with my brother this year." I had noticed that Molly was gone every few Sundays. She had even invited Dwayne and me to come hear her sing in the choir at her brother's church. I knew that she grew up in the Lutheran church, but I hadn't realized that during her first few years in college, she had sort of abandoned church and faith. It wasn't until she saw her brother turn back to church and his faith that it had lit that same fire in her. In the meantime, I wasn't quite sure what going to church had to do with her relationship.

"That's great, Molly! How are you liking it?"

"It's wonderful." She pressed her lips together to subdue a whimper. "I really admire my brother, and it's been amazing to see him go to church even though his friends aren't into Christianity. He says it's really important to him."

We chatted some more, and I waited to see how all of this would lead back to her boyfriend. Finally we hit on it.

She put down her tea and squeezed her hands in the center of her lap. "Well, he's not a Christian, and . . . and I'm not sure if I want to date someone who's not a Christian."

With this, a fresh wave of tears hit her, and her composure crumbled.

I could hear the voices of the youth pastors from my past chorusing their thoughts: "Don't try to missionary date." "It's possible to fall in love with the wrong person." "Don't be unequally yoked." But I knew the time and season in Molly's life for such prescriptive advice was long past.

"What do you feel in your heart you should do?" I asked.

"He's just so wonderful," Molly wept, and I couldn't argue. "He's so kind and good and part of me thinks it doesn't make a difference. But then I also know that my faith is really important to me."

I patted her back, calling to mind a few couples with different faith choices with successful marriages. It's certainly possible to marry someone who doesn't believe what you do, but it's also complicated and adds a level of difficulty I wouldn't want to face in marriage. But these were my own thoughts, not Molly's. I struggled to know what to say, so I reached for a question instead.

"What do your parents say?" I asked.

"They say that marrying someone who doesn't believe the way you do puts a lot of strain on a relationship."

Molly and I spent a couple more hours talking that night. When she left the apartment, I still was not sure what she would choose to do, but I felt good about the fact that I had not handed out advice, but rather supported her in her own decision-making process.

I have spent far too many meaningful conversations giving people advice only to discover that my advice was short-sighted or ill-informed. I have watched as my own choices for life have fit like lumpy, awkward clothes on another person, and I was learning enough about good company by that point to know that what Molly needed in that moment was not another outside voice telling her what to do. What she needed was to learn how to find her own personal conviction in the midst of the many perspectives and voices around her about relationships, dating, faith, and love.

A week or two later, Molly chose to break up with her boyfriend. "It's been really hard," she told me one afternoon, "but I also feel free in a way."

I watched as Molly went into her senior year of college, flourishing in every sense. She continued to go to church with her brother, worked her second year as a resident advisor, and completed her first semester of student teaching.

I caught up with Molly by phone earlier this year. Two years out of college, she lives in Seattle and works as a teacher's assistant. I asked her how things were going and who she felt was being good company for her now in this new phase of life.

"I've started going to a church down here," she explained, her voice lit with a smile. "There's a ton of people my own age: career, post-college," she said. She's joined a running group and a music group and has found in that body of faith a vibrant and lively group of other young adults.

"It's been nice to be around peers going through similar things and who have similar values as me." Her church seems to have become a form of good company for Molly. They walk with her, talk with her, share the ups and downs of the post-college transition, but they also provide a safe space for her to work out the nuances and complexities of her world.

"It's a community that asks questions and gets people thinking," she told me.

In the fertile ground of such good company, Molly has been hashing out her own values, her own personal convictions. She has been discerning what will create the leafy stalk of her life. Molly is living out the second principle of Marcia Baxter

Magolda's theory of good company: "Self is central to knowledge construction."[2] What Magolda means by this is that, although we see that knowledge is created by society, there is also a very real way in which we are in charge of what we will believe. With the help of good company, not just flesh-and-blood good company, but the partnership of the Holy Spirit, we are able to construct the guiding values of life.

Molly shared with me what she has discovered are the core values that create the ethos of her life: First, she is learning that community, openness, and questions are very important to her. She also values the way people are treated. "I value how I speak to people, no matter who they are," she told me. "I think respect is important and that comes from my faith. I believe we are all God's children." Molly also values being grateful no matter what the situation, good or bad. In her experience being deeply rooted in her faith and relationship with Jesus helps her get through both bountiful and tough situations. Finally, Molly is learning that she values integrity and trying to do her best. "No one is perfect," she told me. "But I believe in being honest and doing the best that I can." Molly attributes these values as coming from her relationship with God, and her church has offered her the kind of challenge and support that allows her to wrestle with the complexity of life and find her foundation in the midst of shifting sands.

Being able to articulate these values has also helped shape her decisions in life. It's led her to being a teacher and pursuing a career in service. It's also started to shape her approach toward dating. She told me, "As my faith has become more important, I'm trying to decide if that is important in the people I date." She still doesn't have any firm answers about this. Although Molly has decided that her faith is very important to her, she understands that faith is a very nuanced part of someone's identity. "I want to have grace for people to figure out their own spiritual journey." She's still hashing out just what role faith and spirituality should play in her romantic relationships.

Molly is a beautiful picture of what working through our own personal convictions can look like in the middle of a complex and relativistic world. She understands that not everyone will arrive at the same opinions, beliefs, and convictions that she has, but that hasn't distracted her from her own search for meaning. Day by day, question by question, she is finding her own bit of identity to stand on.

7

BROKEN GLASS

I laid in bed crippled with pain, curled over onto my left side pressing on the side of my abdomen that felt as if shattered glass tore through my flesh. Was this the baby? Was this something I had eaten again? The green light of my bedside clock lit the room with a miserable announcement: 4:30 a.m. I was five months pregnant and alone. Dwayne was away on the other side of the country at a conference, Noelle was asleep in her bedroom, and I needed to get to the emergency room. Who could I call at this time in the morning?

Roughly thirteen weeks into my pregnancy, I had started to develop shattered-glass pain in my abdomen. Dwayne had rushed me to the ER only to find that nothing was wrong. The doctors shot me full of morphine and sent me home. "It could be your gall bladder," the ER doctor offered. "Sometimes, in pregnancy, a woman's gall bladder becomes infected."

I clung to this thread of an explanation with all I had in me. I spent my days researching cleansing drinks and gall-bladder safe food. I gulped concoctions of olive oil and lemon juice, slurped down dishes of lentils and beans full of fiber. Still nothing helped. Out of the blue, I got what I could best describe as "stomach attacks." They most often started gradually in the late afternoon and progressed until I was rigid with pain and motionless on my side.

Even though my stomach was getting slowly larger and larger, I was shedding pounds from my limbs and face until I actually weighed less than before I had gotten pregnant. It was in this state that Dwayne had, with hesitation, left me to go on a conference. "Are you sure you're going to be OK?" he asked, worry creasing his forehead.

I was feeling OK that day. No stomach attacks yet. "Yes, you need to go," I told him. "I'll just call the RAs if I get into trouble."

Well, here I was in trouble, at 4:30 in the morning. I hated to do it, but I knew I needed to wake up Emily, as well as another one of our sweet RAs. Jaqi miraculously answered the phone as soon as she saw my name.

"What's up?" she asked groggily.

"I need to go to the ER. Could you come sleep with Noelle while I go?"

In a few moments Jaqi was at my door, her silky brown hair framing thick-rimmed glasses. I called Emily, who also answered her phone. I had rarely felt such relief and gratitude before in my life.

"Of course!" Emily chirped when I asked if she would mind driving me to the ER since I didn't think I could make it on my own.

I hobbled out into the dark morning by her side, gripping her shoulder as she helped me slide into the passenger seat of her car.

The truth is, those RAs I befriended during our time in Bellingham were as much good company for me as I was for them. There was no room for me to be an authority figure in their lives, or even a mentor, when I spent so much of my time relying on them for help. That first year, while I was pregnant, the girls came and cooked for me, watched Noelle, and cared for me when I had no family around to do it.

What I offered them in the way of guidance had less to do with any sage wisdom on my part than a give-and-take of support on both our parts. Marcia Baxter Magolda writes about this type of collaboration in her third principle of the learning partnership model. She says that good company works with us, that they teach us to share expertise and authority.[1] She writes that the process of helping each other this way involves "collaboration, exchanging and critiquing multiple perspectives, and joint thinking in the process of deciding which perspectives to personally endorse."[2] We can see through this quote that we learn to solve our problems by engaging with [others'] perspectives and insights.

It would take me six months of pain and weight loss before I had a hint of what was making me so sick. In the meantime, the girls and I slugged our way through that school year. As it would turn out, while I was having a physically difficult year, Emily was having an emotionally difficult year. She was a senior, on the verge of graduating, and found herself sinking beneath the work load of studies and being a resident advisor. Other RAs were keeping up with the twenty hours a week of work on top of their classes, but Emily felt as if an anchor had been tied to her feet and she was sinking.

I remember at the end of the year it seemed as if Emily was hobbling toward the finish line. Classes ended, the students started moving out, but Emily still had three or four papers to finish. Her professors had mercy, telling her that she could turn projects in late or make up points with other papers, but she still struggled. Meanwhile, the residence hall was shutting down, Emily needed to move out, but her room was nowhere close to being packed up.

Finally, on the very last day that she could stay in the dorm, she sent a desperate text to Dwayne asking if he could help her move her books and bookshelf out of her room. He found her in tears, completely overwhelmed. He and another colleague came to Emily's rescue. They helped her pack up her belongings and move over to summer housing.

"Poor Emily," Dwayne said to me afterwards. "She's having a breakdown."

It would take another year before Emily finally gave herself grace and recognized that the shaming voices in her head telling her that she was lazy were wrong. Something deeper was going on with her, something that eclipsed the sun from every part of her life: depression. Something I was also battling at the time, but for very different reasons.

After graduation, Emily moved to Anacortis, a small seaport town on the coast of Washington, to work for Americorp. Dwayne and I waved her off and wished her luck. I was going to miss Emily. We stayed in touch through social media and e-mail.

And from time to time, she drove back up to Bellingham to visit friends and come have dinner with us.

It was clear that she wasn't happy, and my heart broke for her. After eleven months of growing steadily more miserable, calling in sick multiple times, dreading work, and beating herself up for feeling like a failure, Emily finally wrote an e-mail to her mom.

In her letter, she explained all that she was feeling, all that she was going through. She told her mom how much she had been struggling the last two years and that she was going to quit her job the next day. She asked if she could move home.

"I remember feeling relieved when I sent the e-mail," Emily told me. "And much more relieved when I got the e-mail back from my mom saying, 'Of course.'" By writing that letter, Emily finally admitted to herself that she was struggling. Finally, she realized something needed to change.

At home in another small town in the countryside of Western Washington, Emily slowly worked to put together the pieces of her fractured two years. Chehalis is a rural city situated along the long rope of the 5 freeway that courses its way from Washington all the way down to California. Mount St. Helens perches on the horizon of Chehalis, skirted in every direction by rolling green landscapes. A friend and fellow staff member at Western, Ashley, visited Emily often.

One afternoon, during a trip to visit Emily, Ashley and Emily were bundled up on the couch in the living room. Outside, a gentle northwest rain hung against the windows like a kiss.

"I don't know whether or not I should regret senior year," Emily said thoughtfully, pushing her feet deeper into the couch. Ashley turned thoughtful eyes toward her.

"Have you been talking to your mom about it?"

Emily nodded, and turned toward the screen. "It's just weird to think I've been depressed these last two years."

Ashley waited a moment and then said, "Where do you think it came from?"

In retrospect, looking back on that conversation, Emily realizes how collaborative Ashley's questions were, how she neither tried to tell Emily what she should do nor what she should feel, but rather asked her questions and then simply shared her own experience with depression.

"What do you think you need?" Ashley asked her. "What do you think about having depression? What do you think you can do?" These types of questions, coupled with her sharing her own story are a great example of how Ashley was more than just a great friend to Emily—she was and continues to be good company.

Emily told me once that some of her close friends frustrate her because they fall on extremes. Some have opinions about everything, and always want everything on their terms, even down to where they hang out, while others are mute, position-less, and never make a decision. With Ashley, it's different. "I never feel like she's trying to fix me," Emily shared.

Now, I have to be honest and confess that Ashley did not just stumble intuitively into being good company for Emily. Both Emily and Ashley had training as a part of the residence life staff at Western Washington University around self-authorship and good company. So Ashley knows what she's doing when she's asking Emily the questions she asks and when she withholds the urge to direct Emily. But what makes Ashley so remarkable is that she's able to embody what she's learned in such an organic way.

It's a gift I think all of us are trying to lean into as good com-pany. How do we hold our own identity while also inviting others to collaborate with us and help us discover our own perspectives on the world?

That early morning, when I was five months pregnant and in the middle of another crippling stomach attack, Emily slipped her arm around me. The sky was still dark. I barely remember the cool breath of moist air against my body. What I remember most was the pain of broken glass, shattering my concentration, my rest, my peace. I leaned into Emily's shoulder and wobbled my way down the hill to the parking lot.

Emily waited for me while the ER doctors ran their ultrasounds over my gut, looking at the baby, looking at my gallbladder, my appendix. "Everything looks in order," the doctor announced skimming my results. I lay on my left side, barely covered by the hospital gown and thin woven blanket. He prescribed a painkiller and sent me home.

Back in the residence hall, I lay in our bed, hardly able to move, my body drained by pain, prescription drugs, and a broken night's sleep. In the other room, Jaqi played with Noelle. She stayed through the morning, cooked me minestrone soup for lunch, and lined up a list of RAs who could come watch Noelle for me the rest of the day. Their voices floated to me through the walls, muted and bustling. I heard Noelle laughing. I heard doors opening and closing. I clung to a thread of gratitude, pulled my way through the day on that thread, until I was finally able to stand at dinnertime and move into the living room. I found Emily and Jaqi laughing with Noelle over a drawing they were creating together. There was no way—there would never be any way—I could thank them enough for all they were doing for me. I leaned into their presence, surrendered to the help they offered me. In so many ways, I should have been the one helping them, mentoring them, leading them through the rocky terrain of college. Instead, we were walking through it together.

8

GLUTEN FREE

"I'm going to send you to a nutritionist because you need to start gaining weight." My ob-gyn looked at me with worried eyes. He was a jolly older gentleman with gray hair and a bow tie, on the cusp of retirement. With that worried look and a flick of his pen, he scheduled for me to meet with a nutritionist associated with the hospital. "I want her to tell us what you can eat." I was now eight months pregnant, and although the little boy inside my womb was growing healthy and strong, my doctor was afraid that if I continued to lose weight, the baby's health would also be compromised.

I nodded my head and lifted my skeletal frame off the examining table, proceeding with my swollen belly out the door.

A few days later, I sat in the nutritionist's office surrounded by more books and fliers than I'd ever seen in one small space. Beside me, Noelle played with a basket of plastic fruit, bread, and meat. She proceeded to make for me a very thick sandwich complete with grapes and sausage wedged between the slices of bread. The nutritionist sat across from me, the light from the large window lighting her hair. "So tell me what you've been eating."

I pulled two folded pages out of my bag and spread them out across her desk. On each page I had the meal plan of the previous two weeks. Her bright eyes scanned over the menus. I scooted forward in my chair and reached toward the pages. "I got sick on this day," I said pointing to the Wednesday when I had prepared tortellini for dinner. "I also got sick on this day," I said running my finger to the next meal of homemade pizza. "But I didn't get sick on this day," I said pointing to the Friday when I had made salmon, brown rice, and salad. With resignation, I flopped back into the chair just in time for Noelle to lift her meal of rubber bread to my lips.

The nutritionist looked over my plans and with hardly a beat said pointedly, "You should definitely eliminate gluten from your diet immediately. I'll send some paperwork over for you to get your blood drawn and see if you have celiac disease."

"What's that?" I asked, a glimmer of hope flitting through my chest. Not that I wanted anything including the word *disease* in its title, but I had been sick for six months, week after week spent living in fear of food, hungry day after day, yet unable to eat without pain. My ob-gyn had no answers for me. Neither did my primary care physician, and even two visits with the gastroenterologist left me without explanation.

"We're not sure what's making you so sick," he had said. "I know you're in a lot of pain, but if you can just bear it until the baby is born, then we'll run our tests." Of course I would wait until the baby was born. No matter how much pain I was in, I would never knowingly do anything to endanger the eggplant-sized little boy growing inside me. I went home resigned to live through another three months of debilitating pain.

I did not walk into the nutritionist's office that day looking for an answer to the pain, as much as I was looking for food. Even though I was plagued by stomach pain nearly every hour of the day, I was also hungry, hungry to my bones. The prospect of having a diagnosis and thereby finally getting answers was thrilling. Eliminate gluten. Celiac disease. Suddenly, someone was saying words that sounded like an explanation.

"The wheat we eat today is vastly different from the wheat our grandmothers cooked with," the nutritionist explained.

She leaned back in her chair with an easy air, as if she was not looking at a woman on the verge of despair, wracked by hunger and pain. I wanted to shake her and say, "This is serious! Don't smile so much! Can't you see I'm sick?"

And still she drawled on in her even tone. "Our bodies aren't meant to process the amount of gluten genetically engineered into our wheat. Most people do fine, but then there are others, the canaries, who suffer."

Noelle handed me a plate of fake spaghetti and I suddenly saw it with new eyes. Ironic. In my attempts to assuage the pain, I had cut everything out of my diet except for oatmeal and toast, thinking those foods would be safe. In reality, they were possibly making me even sicker.

I greedily took the thick red folder the nutritionist gave me, packed with information on gluten allergies and celiac disease. "I might have celiac disease," I spoke breathlessly over the phone to my mother.

"What does that mean?" my mom asked. And I explained as best I could from the nutritionist's words.

"It means no flour, no bread, no pasta. I guess I can do corn and rice. I have lots more reading to do!"

By the end of the first day without gluten, I could sense a shift in my body. By the end of day three, a miracle had happened.

After living for six months with inexplicable pain, only made worse by the aches and nausea of pregnancy, I was finally pain free. Just like that, without any drugs or tests or surgeries. A simple elimination diet cured me. By the end of the week, I had more energy than I'd had since before I had gotten pregnant. Dwayne and I went to Trader Joe's and pillaged their gluten-free granola and corn pasta. We stopped by the local Fred Meyer where I spent hours staring at the gluten-free aisle devouring with my eyes all the foods I had been denied for the last three months: gingersnap cookies, macaroons, pancakes, homemade bread. I ate three and four helpings at each meal and gloried in the satisfaction of no broken glass in my gut.

I waited anxiously for my blood results to come in. Wordlessly, I hoped with nearly a pathological fervor that I had celiac disease. As absurd as this sounds, I felt I needed a definitive medical answer to validate the last six months of pain I had endured. Without that validation, I worried that perhaps I was just overreacting, working myself into a tizzy over something that any other woman could endure with grace. I was certain that, without the doctor's diagnosis, others would think I was simply being high maintenance.

"Why do you think that?" Dwayne asked me with a tinge of irritation in his voice. I sat in a puddle of tears, bawling and bawling because, just that afternoon, the doctor had called, and my test results had come back negative. I did not have celiac disease. "Just because the doctor's say you don't have celiac disease, doesn't mean something's not wrong with you. I mean, look how much better you're doing after taking out gluten? That's not a figment of your imagination."

To hear him validate me and my six months of suffering as more than a weak woman exaggerating was a comfort, and I took it in pieces, trying to calm down. In truth, after fighting my body for half the year, the long finger of depression was already starting to tap on the door of my heart, though I couldn't yet see it. I was mentally and emotionally worn down, even now that the physical pain was relieved. I had no buoyancy, no way to cope with bad news or disappointment.

"Not having celiac disease is a good thing," the nutritionist chuckled on the other end of the phone. The lightness in her voice irritated me. I wanted her to take all of this as seriously as I was. "It means you don't have to worry about having a particle or speck of gluten. If you get a crumb of toast on the same knife you're buttering your gluten-free toast, you'll be fine."

"But just having a sensitivity to gluten can still result in all the pain I've been in?" I asked feebly.

"Yes," the nutritionist said. "It can cause the kinds of reactions you're having. The gold standard for knowing if you have a sensitivity to gluten is simply eliminating it from your diet and seeing how you feel."

Well, there was no denying it. I felt rejuvenated. The evaporation of pain from my gut sent my body soaring. It felt so good not to hurt.

"Why do you need the doctor's validation?" Dwayne had asked me when I was in my fit of despair over not having celiac disease. I couldn't quite answer his question. His words clipped ahead of me then bounced back to echo through my psyche.

I felt I needed an expert's diagnosis because I didn't yet trust my own capacity to know when I was healthy and when I was not. This type of knowing felt outside of me, ethereal and intangible. How could it be enough to simply trust my body? Couldn't I be tricking myself? Couldn't I be weak and overreacting like I had done over and over again as a little girl?

Dwayne's question pushed me to wrestle with my own capacity to know. He was enacting Marcia Baxter Magolda's fourth principle of learning partnerships: Good company validates the learner's capacity to know.[1] I was not just an empty vessel that could be told by the doctors whether or not I was sick. I knew, deep in my body that I was sick, and I needed to learn to trust that knowing and to move toward a plan of health whether or not any doctors ever recognized how sick I was.

Dr. John Purdie explained this fourth principle of learning partnership to me further. He said, "When a student says, 'The sky is gray,' you don't say, 'No it's not. It's blue!' You respect, honor, and take as valid what [a person's] own experience is."[2] In other words, validating someone's capacity to know means respecting his or her particular understanding of the world at that moment, regardless of your own perspective on the matter.

I see this all the time with the freshmen that I teach now. As a part of my course, we work through articles and videos that deal with difference and the "other." We talk about white privilege, straight privilege, and socioeconomic privilege. These conversations inevitably get heated, but they also engender an amazing sense of camaraderie in my classes. It's fascinating to watch my students learn to voice their own biases and opinions and to greet each other with challenge, but also empathy. They are beginning to piece together their own sense of authority about issues like racism on campus, minimum wage laws, and sexual objectification in the media.

In the same way, I was still learning, eight years out of college, how to trust my own capacity to know. By asking me why I felt I needed the doctor's validation, Dwayne forced me to acknowledge my own experience and to trust my ability to know at a fundamental level. We weren't dealing with heady identity theories. I wasn't trying to grasp my ability to know in a transcendent way. I was taking baby steps, learning to trust my ability to know in the most basic and physical of ways: my health and the wellness of my own body.

9

LOVING SPACE

I pulled up in front of the sweet little red house. Sunflowers lolled happily over the edge of the fence, grinning as I walked past. Along the fence etched into the wood were children's handprints with names inside: Torsten, Horace, Skya, Ellis, Marley. I reached the purple door and pushed it open. Inside, a thrum of little voices, laughing and chattering, washed over me. I loved this preschool already and knew I wanted Noelle to go here.

"Are you Christin?" A head of crazy brown curls bounced toward me. "I'm Sherry! The director." Sherry and I shook hands. "Let me give you a tour," Sherry exclaimed, and I followed her into a large room to the right. Essentially, Loving Space was a house that had been renovated into a preschool. The children ran freely through the downstairs in a steady stream of directed chaos.

In the center of the "Big Room" (as it was called), a large tire swing carved into the shape of a horse galloped back and forth. In one corner, moldable dots covered a large table. In another corner, the room ducked into a smaller space where the children could paint the walls whatever color or pattern that spiked their little minds.

In the other half of the house, Sherry showed me the "Quiet Room." This room was sectioned by a large overstuffed couch where the kids could lie down and listen to stories. In another corner lived a black gerbil and other small scurrying animals. To the left, a small cluster of children played with a magnifying camera, holding the lens up to their hands and faces, the table, their clothes, watching as the pores of their skin suddenly morphed into textures of abstract art on the TV monitor. In the back of the house, an entire room was engulfed by a climbing set with a slide and boxes of dress-up clothes. Princesses, monsters, pirates, and animals crawled over the play set in a scramble of activity.

Outside, kids whizzed past my head on a zip line, while others poured buckets of pink, green, and blue water into test tubes and bowls. I watched as one little boy drenched himself in water. Sherry followed my eyes and then smiled. "We ask that you don't send Noelle to school in clothes you don't want to get dirty. We don't believe in having the kids wear smocks or aprons. We want them to feel fully invited into their environment. So we have you send a spare set of clothes to school that we keep on hand in case we need a change." I nodded, and took a step further down the side of the house where the zip line whipped to its end. There, I found a tree fort, like something out of Neverland. Children scrambled up and over branches getting higher and higher. Around the circumference of the tree was netting in case they should fall.

Suddenly, a shriek pierced the air. I spun around to see two children yanking at a particular jug of purple water. Sherry glided into action. She knelt beside them and spoke in an even voice. "Do you all need some help here?"

The children stopped, stunned by her easy presence, her reasonable address. Slowly, the panic in their little bodies melted and they shook their heads. "She keeps pushing me out of the way," the little boy motioned toward the girl.

"Skya, Ellis is making it clear that he doesn't want you to push him out of the way. Is there another way you could ask to play with the water?"

I watched stunned as the little girl nodded her head and stepped out of the way. She placed her little hand on Ellis's shoulder and said, "Can I have a turn when you're done?"

How was this even possible? I had never seen children react so reasonably to an adult. What sort of food were they feeding these kids? I was certain, Noelle would never deescalate out of a tantrum that smoothly.

"Noelle is going to love that place," I told Dwayne that evening. And in fact, nothing was truer. For the first two months of Noelle's stay at Loving Space, she threw a tantrum every time I came to pick her up. I quickly got in the habit of showing up with lollipops so as to bribe her away from this wonderful house that engulfed her world in fun and learning.

"We want to share with you a bit about our pedagogy," Abby, the founder and creator of Loving Space, said on our first night of parent orientation. Dwayne and I sat shoulder to shoulder on a small red wooden bench meant for little legs. A crowd of adults packed into the Big Room in order to listen to Abby's presentation. The wild tire horse had been removed to make room for the parents that now huddled on benches, pillows, and little square rugs.

Abby was gorgeous in the way that makes you want to watch her for hours on end. Like Sherry, she had a crop of curls bursting from her heart-shaped face, an adorable gap between her front teeth, and a quiet voice that pulled you in. "We have something for you," she grinned. Sherry moved to a bunch of brown paper bags on the corner and began passing them out. "We picked these just this week from a local orchard," Abby said as the paper bags made their way through our hands. I reached in and found a pile of apples, stems and leaves still attached. "Take one!" Abby encouraged, and we each pulled out an apple.

"OK," Abby said, holding a marker in her hand and turning toward a massive piece of blank paper taped to the wall behind her. "Hold the apple, feel it, smell it, taste it. Tell me everything you experience. Just shout it out."

The parents giggled and sat awkwardly for a moment, unsure of how to proceed. "Red!" a brave soul began.

"Right! Red," Abby wrote the word up on the board.

"Green!" "Round." "Crisp." "Leaves." "Sweet." "Worm holes." "Bruises." The words tumbled out from the group, until we had a list that covered the page from top to bottom.

"Alright," Abby turned to Sherry and nodded. "We have something else for you." Sherry passed around a bag of plastic apples. We all took one, holding the waxy orbs in our palms. "Now tell me, which descriptors still apply?"

I looked at the list, scanning over the words. *Crisp* and *sweet* needed to be taken down, as well as *bruises* and *worm holes*. Other words trickled off the list that could not be experienced through a fake apple. Next, Abby took the fake apples away from us and then showed us a picture of an apple.

"Now, which words still apply to this apple?" Again, more words came off the list until just a few remained: *round*, *red*, *fruit*. Finally, Abby removed even the picture of the word and held up a piece of cardboard with just the word *apple* printed across it. "And what words still apply to this?" Nothing remained from the list, because there was no experience to associate directly with the word *apple*, except for what we had felt, touched, and tasted with the real thing. The black-and-white print was a symbol, an abstract sign that we could only attach to the real, live, organic apples we had held in our hands just a few minutes before.

"This is why we do experiential learning here at Loving Space," Abby explained. "Our goal is to generate as many experiences as possible for your children. These experiences will become hooks in their mind that they can later hang their learning on."

If I had not been sold on Loving Space before, at that moment, I was. "That's brilliant!" I chirped to Dwayne as we made our way home. I kept envisioning the tiny hooks in Noelle's brain upon which she would one day be ready to hang the abstract concepts of math and writing and reading.

I had no idea then that I was witnessing in that preschool space the tangible expression of Marcia Baxter Magolda's fifth principle of learning partnerships. She writes that good company "situates learning in the learner's experience."[1] In other words, good company knows that active learning happens best when it comes out of our own experiences with the world. How brilliant were Abby, Sherry, and the rest of the Loving Space teachers? They were doing for our children, at a very early age, what I hope we can all find in our young adult years.

The National Association of Student Affairs Professionals writes, "Active learning invites students to bring their life experiences into the learning process, reflect on their own and others' perspectives as they expand their viewpoints, and apply new understandings to their own lives."[2] In other words, our experiences, both good and bad, successes and failures, form the foundation of our learning, and good company knows this. For that reason, good company doesn't only validate our capacity to know, but also creates space for us to bring our experiences to the learning table.

By providing Noelle and the other kids at Loving Space the opportunity to experience the look of their skin and clothes through the magnification camera, Abby and Sherry were providing a catalogue of memories that the students could later take to their science classes. By recycling live Christmas trees after Christmas and creating a forest of evergreens in the back yard of the preschool, Abby created a magical world where stories could come to life. By talking to the kids as if they were human beings, Sherry and the teachers taught the children not to be intimidated by adults, but to speak to parents and teachers with confidence and respect.

By the time we left Bellingham, I would have happily stayed just to have Noelle continue her education at Loving Space's kindergarten. "I wish they had a Loving Space middle school all the way up to high school," I told Dwayne one evening after we had visited the kindergarten orientation. "What would a Loving Space high school even look like?" I mused with a chuckle.

The truth is, good company enacts the Loving Space pedagogy every time it allows us to pull from our own experiences in order to learn. Every time we are asked, "What is that experience like for you? How is it working for you?" it assumes first, that we have the ability to interpret our experiences for ourselves, and second, that those experiences can shape the construction of our future in meaningful and satisfying ways, aside from the voice of an outside authority.

When asked why the school was called Loving Space, one of the children replied, "Because kids need love, and they need space." Abby thought this answer was so brilliant that she made it into a poster and put it up in the entryway of the little house. I couldn't agree more. All of us need love, and all of us need space to learn from our experiences.

10

DEPRESSION

How long the spindly fingers of depression had been tangling my heart, mind, and soul I wasn't sure, but I thought I could perhaps trace them back to our move to Bellingham. After all, as much as I enjoyed living in Bellingham, there was no denying the loss upon loss that transition meant for me: no work, no family close by, no friends. Then a few months after our arrival I had gotten pregnant, then miserably and doggedly sick with pain.

"Chronic pain makes you feel totally isolated," my friend Mandy shared with me one afternoon as I cried into the receiver of my phone. Mandy's voice reached me soothing and quiet from the Midwest. Having battled her own chronic pain for years,

Mandy was uniquely empathetic. "John and I are so sorry for you, Christin," she said. "We are praying for you!"

The warmth of her voice wrapped me up like two strong arms, and in their embrace my composure dissolved. I bawled and bawled, wordless and breathless. Every day was a fresh fight against my body, and every day I rose to the fight as best I could — put on a brave face and met the demands of my rambunctious three-year-old. Yet the broken glass in my stomach was getting worse. Whereas the glass had appeared perhaps once every couple weeks in the beginning, now it had taken up residence in my tender abdomen on a regular basis. I doubled over in pain nearly every day around dinner time. Dwayne had grown accustomed to coming home from work to a crippled wife, curled up on the couch or bed, while Noelle watched TV shows on the computer — the best I could do to keep her entertained while I suffered.

"I'm sorry, I couldn't even start dinner," I told Dwayne for the fifth night in a row. His chin sunk down to his chest and he slumped off to the kitchen, disappointed and worried.

"You know, I had to go on antidepressants while I was pregnant," Mandy said lightly. "Maybe you should consider it."

I listened, but somewhere inside me a fist of resistance tightened. No, I wasn't depressed. I was just sick. As soon as this pain went away, I would be fine.

The weeks marched on, and I pulled myself along with white knuckles thinking that perhaps relief was just around the corner, that perhaps this pain would go away and I could return to normal. But each day, the stomach attacks returned and like one of those inflatable toys you kick or hit and they swing back to standing, I was starting to slowly deflate. I bounced back less and less, and each time I came up a shrunken version of myself.

By that point, we had found a church and small group in Bellingham that we liked very much. One Sunday evening, after small group, I decided it was time to share with them just how much I was struggling and ask for their prayers. During prayer time, I got perhaps two words into my request and puddled into tears. Dwayne stepped in and explained just what was happening, and our group, with eyes full of care, circled around me to pray.

"You know, I had to go on antidepressants when I was pregnant," my head snapped up, echoing with the same sentence Mandy had spoken to me a few weeks before. Only this time, the confession came from the mouth of a pretty, young mom on the other side of the circle, Georgianne. Her eyebrows knit together and she proceeded gently. "It really helped me, and I know Dr. Fergeson has a great relationship with a psychiatrist." Upon the utterance of his name, my mind conjured up the image of

Dr. Fergeson, my ob-gyn, his jolly face and bow tie. Suddenly, a memory bubbled to the surface, one I had dismissed at the time.

In the memory, I sat on his examining table after a routine visit, and he looked at me carefully.

"I'm worried about you," he had said. "You're suffering a lot. If you feel you ever need to talk to someone about the blues, I have a great psychiatrist who works with me. I can get you an appointment with Julie right away."

"Thank you," I said and slipped my way off the table and out into the gray and rainy afternoon, dismissing his suggestion. I was fine. I was just in pain. I didn't need medication for anything other than my pain. As soon as that went away, I would be fine.

Back in the small group, I held Giorgianne's suggestion that I talk to Dr. Fergeson at arm's length, but at least considered it a bit more than Mandy's suggestion. Perhaps, there might come a time when I needed to consider psychiatric help, but surely I wasn't that bad yet. After all, the major symptoms I associated with depression didn't apply to me. I wasn't considering suicide. I certainly would eat if I could. And my troubles with sleep had more to do with my pain and pregnancy than any mood disorders.

As I look back now on that first year in Bellingham, I'm stunned it took me so long, and so many brushes with others' suggestions before I recognized the symptoms of depression in myself. But perhaps these things are not so easily embraced. Depression, cloaked as it is in stigma, is a scary thing to look in the face. My family had dealt with anxiety for generations, and we had always handled it just fine with the help of nothing more than prayer. Surely I was not that broken, I told myself. I did not need to stoop to medicine for help, although if I were honest, I did not think that Mandy or Giorgianne were weak, and they had turned to antidepressants. Somehow, my resistance toward getting help was completely internalized.

It's a wonder that I didn't recognize all the subtle flags of help that shot up around me during those months. Mandy, Giorgianne, and Dr. Fergeson, all completely independent of one another, were not the only ones to speak to me about depression. All the way in Hungary, on the opposite side of the world lived Gwen, a spunky, soft-spoken woman the same age as my mother. Gwen and her husband were working overseas for a season as missionaries. I had met Gwen through one of my college friends. "I think you and my mom would love each other!" he told me. "She loves to write, but she needs something and someone to write for."

Gwen and I had never met face-to-face, but during those two years in Bellingham, we cultivated a rich friendship over e-mail and Skype. Gwen and I did indeed love each other. We were generations apart, and yet kindred spirits. I encouraged her in her writing and she encouraged me in my journey as a young mother. Gwen had raised four children all a year or two apart and she understood intimately the demands of such a life. She had also just gone through a major transition of her own, having left behind her well-manicured life in the Midwest and moving to Hungary. Her children were all grown now with children of their own, and she and her husband were uniquely free to pursue a stint of missions work. We shared with each other the ups and downs of such a transition, of moving to a place where family and friends were so far away.

During this time, she shared with me honestly about her own battle with depression. "I'm feeling so much better now that I've been on antidepressants for three weeks. I feel like a new person. I've been doing quite a bit of reading on depression. It's been very helpful in understanding how depression works." I devoured her e-mails. Though unwilling to admit that I was struggling with depression myself, her admissions and insights nourished me.

While she was moving through healing, she very thoughtfully and gently shared her learning with me, as if she suspected I was myself in depression. She refused to say as much, but rather opted to share what she was learning, leaving it to me to construct my own understanding around her stories.

"Depression is almost always caused by loss, which includes grief," she wrote me one day as she explained all she was learning through her reading and through the Christian counselor she had found in Hungary. Yes, I could relate to this. As I tallied up the past year, there was much I had lost: work, friends, family, my health. I wondered if perhaps all these losses had taken a larger toll on my buoyancy than I had first imagined.

"Oh, Christin, I have great hope for you," she wrote me as I began to share the depths of panic and despair I felt mingling each day. "If you are indeed experiencing depression, there is a solution. Healing and restoration is on its way!"[1]

My final breaking point came on a rare sunny morning in early spring. By this point, we had discovered that gluten was the cause of all my pain, and I had begun the elimination diet, which also eliminated my pain; however, it did not eliminate the great cloud of sadness which had come to cling to me like the Pacific Northwest mist.

For two nights earlier that week, I had managed to shake the sadness late in the evening. In fact, the night before, Dwayne and I had a lovely evening together, laughing and chatting after Noelle went to bed, talking about the upcoming birth of our son. I was about thirty-five weeks pregnant by that point, and we were turning our attention toward the details of labor and delivery.

"Good," I thought as I went to bed that night. "It's been a good night. Tomorrow, I won't wake up feeling sad. The pain is gone. Life can get back to normal."

The next morning, I loaded Noelle up in the car, and we headed out to Lake Padden Park, one of our favorite spots to play. I directed the car down the winding road that threaded us through green leafy trees to the little haven of a lake nestled between lush hills. The sun pierced down through the leaves like lace, and suddenly my heart dropped. For no explicable reason, I felt sad again. It was almost as if the sadness were outside of me, as if it had spirited its way into the passenger seat of the car and was leaning against me like an old friend. "Oh, there you are," I thought almost reflexively. "You're back."

At that moment, red and blue lights flashed behind me. I gasped and looked up into the rearview mirror to see a cop flagging me down. I took a quick glance at my speedometer only to see that while I was so deeply drawn into thought, my foot had pushed heavy on the gas pedal, and I was flying down the road about fifteen miles over the speed limit. My throat tightened, and I pulled over.

"Do you know how fast you were going, miss?" the police officer asked as I rolled down the window. His eyes swept over my great belly and Noelle sitting in the back seat. I nodded contritely. "Do you know what the speed limit is here?" I nodded my head again, and felt tears burning up like hot lava. In that moment, I despised myself. The last thing I wanted to do was cry in front of this police officer like a lousy, weak pregnant mother of a preschooler. I choked and tried to force the tears back down.

The police officer's face softened as he looked back down at my swollen stomach. "Well," he said. "I know they don't post the speed limit on this road, and I know you're not going to speed again. Let's just call this a warning. Have a good day, miss."

My face burned with shame and relief. I nodded and squeaked out a "Thank you, officer."

As soon as he disappeared, I wrenched the window up and bawled and bawled. "Are you OK, Mommy?" Noelle crooned from the back. I watched as the police officer's car sailed around me and into the bend in the trees.

"No, I'm not OK," I admitted to Noelle, surrendering to the wash of tears and snot flowing from every orifice on my face. My thoughts spun forward. "If I was just not living in a residence hall, I would be OK," I thought. "If I just weren't pregnant, I would be OK." The ifs marched on. "If I were just not about to have a baby and go into sleepless nights and months of breast-feeding, I would be OK." Suddenly, I came up short. I gripped the steering wheel and looked up. Suddenly, I saw myself from a bird's-eye view. My mind floated somewhere above the car, looking down at myself.

"What are you talking about?" my out-of-body self asked. "If you weren't about to have a baby, you would be OK? This is your life! This is what you have chosen! If you were to talk to yourself two years ago, you would be so happy to have a baby, so excited! Your dad calls you his 'sunshine girl.' This isn't you. You're not this person, sad all the time, panicked all the time, and so full of despair."

In that moment, I pulled the car out of park, turned it around and drove straight to Dr. Fergeson's office. In a matter of a few days, I had an appointment with the psychiatrist, and in another day or two, I had begun taking a low dose of antidepressants.

"This is actually an anti-anxiety medication," the doctor told me with a smile. "You can take it and breastfeed, no problem. The last thing we want you to do is sail off into postpartum land! No way!"

I remember two weeks later, sitting on the counter in our small apartment kitchen, chatting with Dwayne. I forget what we were talking about, but I do remember that halfway through the conversation, Dwayne looked at me and smiled sheepishly. "I think the medicine is working."

I laughed. Yes, I could feel it, just like Gwen had said. The dread was gone. My emotions were stable. I felt like engaging life. I didn't feel elated or extra happy as much as I just felt normal. What a relief to simply feel normal—no pain, no sadness, just the lightness of being.

As I look back at my slow acceptance of depression, I can't help but send up a thousand thankful prayers to God for bringing Mandy, Giorgianne, Dr. Fergeson, and Gwen into my life. All of them seemed to understand intuitively that, though they saw me suffering, they could not force me to go look for help or even tell me to go look for help. Instead, Mandy, Giorgianne, and especially Gwen, understood that the best way to move me forward was to offer their experiences and allow me to attach my experiences to theirs, drawing a bridge between the two and arriving at my own moment of revelation.

The power of their stories was the power of Marcia Baxter Magolda's sixth and final principle of learning partnerships: Good company defines learning as mutually constructed meaning.[2] These women did not tell me what to do. Instead, they walked beside me and worked with me, giving me their insights and experiences in order to help me make sense out of my own experiences. They didn't try to fix me. It must have been so difficult for them to sit back and watch as I continued to struggle despite their efforts, but this is the great test of being good company. After helping us wrestle with the problem, crisis, or question, good company must be willing to let go of the final decision. Good company has to be willing to accept that our answer may be different from theirs. Mandy, Giorgianne, and Gwen had to let go of the fact that I might listen to all they had to share and still walk away from antidepressants and the help they so accurately perceived I needed.

Today, I know and understand not just my body better, but my emotions and psyche better too. I know that depression is a deeply nuanced and complex thing. It doesn't mean that I was about ready to kill myself. It didn't adhere to the stereotypes and stigma I had placed on it all my life. For me, the moment depression became the old friend, lagging with me day after day, that was the moment I opened my arms and embraced it. For me to have continued to ignore it and explain it away would only have been to empower depression and feed it. But for me to see it, recognize it, and acknowledge its presence was the first step in the walk toward freedom.

11

THE HOLY SPIRIT AS GOOD COMPANY

The group pressed around me, their hands reaching out to rest on my shoulders, back, and head. I sat in the middle of the comfortable living room where we had met for the last year in our small group. My friends had gathered around me to pray for me in the midst of my sickness and pain. None of us knew what was going on with me yet, and so our group did the only thing they knew to do for me: They touched me and talked to God on my behalf.

Most of us in the room were young parents with young kids, except for one couple: Ed and Jenny. Their kid was grown and out of the house. Ed had a salt-and-pepper push-broom mustache and played the bass guitar at gigs around town. Jenny was an artist. Their small apartment dining room had been transformed into her studio, stacked with canvases, paints, and brushes. They were a "groovy" couple in their late fifties, and they charged our group with energy and wisdom.

I remember on this particular evening of prayer, when the last voice had quieted and the prayer time was done, Ed reached out a hand, placed it on my shoulder and said, "Christin, I feel like the Lord wants me to tell you that whatever promises he gave you for this season, he will fulfill."

I sat for a moment thunderstruck, letting his words wash over me in waves. With each wave, I slid back in time to a small room on the edge of Biola University's campus. Before I was sick, before I was pregnant, before we moved to Bellingham, I was teaching freshman composition at Biola in a little city situated on the eastern side of Los Angeles. During my time at Biola, I had applied for a grant to do spiritual direction. I had no idea really what this was, only that it was a service provided by Biola's Institute of Spiritual Formation and that an acquaintance of mine had gone through the program and spoke very highly of it.

The first time I walked into my spiritual director's office, I wondered what on earth we would talk about, what we would do. What was this spiritual direction thing anyway?

"Would you like me to explain to you a little bit about spiritual direction, or would you like to just begin and experience it?" My director, Jackie, sat across from me in a large pillow of a recliner. I sat perhaps two feet across from her in a similarly comfortable recliner. The room was tiny. So tiny, I felt we were sitting in a closet, knee to knee.

I kicked her question around in my mind. Which did I want? An explanation or an experience? I looked at her tentatively. She had brown curly hair and bright, piercing eyes. Jackie had previously been a missionary and was married with three children. She had seen the world and lived life. I picked experience.

"Let's just jump in," I said.

In her book, *Holy Listening: The Art of Spiritual Direction*, Margaret Guenther describes what it is that a spiritual director does. She writes, "The director's task is to help connect the individual's story to *the* story and thereby help the directee to recognize and claim identity in Christ, discern the action of the Holy Spirit."[1] In other words, the spiritual director helps us clear away the misconceptions and mend the cracked glass of our inner lens so that we are able to see clearly God's movement in our lives.

Spiritual direction has its roots deep in the church, stretching all the way back to the early Catholic church and the monastic tradition. It is the act of walking with another through his or her spiritual journey. The spiritual director is neither a priest, nor a mentor, nor counselor. He or she is more like a sounding board—an educated listener and question-asker.

Guenther describes the direction relationship this way: "In this covenanted relationship the director has agreed to put [him- or herself] aside so that his [or her] total attention can be focused on the person sitting in the other chair. What a gift to bring to another, the gift of disinterested, loving attention!"[2] The spiritual director provides a space for us to turn our attention inward and to process with them the workings of our spirit, our heart.

I left my time with Jackie that day in a flood of tears. Not angry or bitter tears, but tears that purged my soul. They were a relief, a release. Under Jackie's direction for the next two years, I stumbled month after month onto deep pools of anxiety I had harbored and skirted every day. Our sessions followed this pattern for the first year—me wondering what on earth we had to talk about and then finding myself in a pool of sweet, cleansing tears by the end of the session. "People come to direction burdened with a sense of their own unworthiness and unloveliness, crushing shame, and their own sins."[3] I had no idea how true this was for me. No idea how I walked around everyday clinging to my shame as if it were a birthright and part of my identity.

My time with Jackie unwound in the years following my shipwreck, and my time with her was a valuable asset as I continued to untangle the web of emotions and beliefs that had sprouted up in my heart about God and his love for me during that season of chaos and loss.

"Let's begin with silence," Jackie said to me on that first meeting. "Go inward and see what God has for you today."

And we sat for fifteen minutes in silence. I squirmed uncomfortably, having never been that quiet with anybody in my entire life. And my mind wriggled and leapt about like a restless toddler unwilling to settle. I grasped it and tried to pin it down, worried that I would come out of the silence with nothing from God, nothing to work on.

But always, every single time, something would rise to the top of my brain and Jackie and I would take it and run. Always the sessions would end, and I would be brimming with realizations, frantic to somehow write them down, to capture them, to explain and share them with Dwayne, but I always felt at a loss. You see, I was never quite sure how we had arrived where we arrived, only that I felt somehow more solid, as if I was moving from the shadow of a person to flesh and blood.

I remember at the end of one session, looking at Jackie with shining eyes and proclaiming, "I need to go write this down! I don't want to forget it."

She leaned toward me and smiled, shaking her head. "You don't need to write it down," she said. "The Holy Spirit has given this to you, and what the Spirit's given to you cannot be taken away. The Spirit will remind you when you need to be reminded."

What a beautiful thought. A wave of relief lapped over me. I did not need to be responsible for the truth that was cropping up in my soul. You see, I wasn't alone. I didn't carry it only on my shoulders. I had a helpmate, a companion, moving with me every moment, there to guide, remind, and counsel me.

This is the task of the Holy Spirit. I didn't truly know how to recognize the Holy Spirit's presence in my life until my time with Jackie. She was for me a tangible, physical object lesson of what the Holy Spirit does for us.

In John 14, Jesus revealed to his disciples that he was about to leave them. When he saw the anxiety written all over their faces, he told them not to worry. He said, "I will ask the Father, and He will give you another Helper, that He may be with you forever" (John 14:16 NASB). Jesus said he would ask God to bring them a *paracletos*, someone to walk alongside them. He then described the essence of the Holy Spirit: "But the Helper, the Holy Spirit, whom the Father will send in My name, He will teach you all things, and bring to your remembrance all that I said to you" (John 14:26 NASB).

Over and over again, during my sessions with Jackie, she taught me to recognize the Holy Spirit in my life. I began to see the Spirit clearly, moving alongside me, leading me gently in tangible and loving ways. I often found myself breathless and speechless over the way the Holy Spirit came through for me in the most unexpected ways. I could barely fathom how real the Spirit was in my life.

Guenther sums up for me what Jackie did. She writes to her fellow spiritual directors when she says, "We can help them see the next small, often deceptively simple steps."[4] So much of what Jackie did for me seemed deceptively small and simple from the outside looking in, and yet, my life was changed through our time together in significant ways.

When I went to Jackie at the end of our two years together and told her that Dwayne and I would be moving to Bellingham, Washington, she smiled at me and said, "Thrive. This is the word God is giving me for your time in Washington. It's a time for you to thrive."

Well, that first year certainly did not feel like a time of thriving. Often, when I was curled and hunched over in pain, I remembered Jackie's prophecy, and I buried the word deep down in my subconscious. I told myself she had been wrong. And with an internal sigh of resignation and disappointment, I pushed the word *thrive* out of my mind.

So that evening, when Ed placed his hand on me and told me that the promises God had given me for my time in Bellingham would be fulfilled, the word *thrive* came lurching out of the deep, springing its way back from the dark corner where I had buried it. I sucked in my breath and looked at Ed, his gentle eyes peering down at me from beneath his bushy eyebrows. Fresh tears slid down my cheek.

"OK," I whispered into my soul, to the place where Jackie had taught me to encounter the Holy Spirit. "You said I would thrive here. I believe you."

It's been three years now, since my last session with Jackie, and perhaps what I carry closest to me is the incredible gift she gave me of helping me unearth, like an archeologist, my relationship with the Holy Spirit, which had been dulled and buried beneath the depths of my shame, anxiety, and confusion. This, Guenther says, is the ultimate goal of every spiritual director— to connect their directees to the Holy Spirit, because as she puts it, "The Holy Spirit is the true director."[5] And I might add, the true Good Companion.

The literature and research on learning partnerships stops in the area of spiritual companionship and the Holy Spirit. The academic voices fall silent. There is nothing written, that I've found, about the place of the Holy Spirit in our young adult identity development. Marcia Baxter Magolda talks about being our own good company when we can't find any around us.[6] And while I think this is true, that we can learn to ask ourselves the same kinds of questions a learning partner might, I also think that kind of conversation does not take into consideration the presence of a spiritual dimension to our lives.

Jesus promised to send us the ultimate counselor, the ultimate companion in the gift of the Holy Spirit, and for those of us who follow Jesus, this gift is open to us as we move through our young adult years.

What does it mean for us then, as we navigate our shipwrecks, to have the companionship of the Holy Spirit? What place does the Spirit's still small voice have amidst all the voices in our lives we are trying to sift through? What do we do with this eternal and divine companion as we are on the quest of honing our own internal voice? The best I have to offer you is my own insight and experience.

I believe the process of learning to listen to our own internal voices is not just the exercise of discerning our internal authority. I think it's actually the process of learning how to discern the ongoing dialogue between our internal voice and the voice of the Holy Spirit. There is a conversation happening, and we are welcome to tune in.

I would add to Marcia Baxter Magolda's research by saying that there is not actually one voice that we listen to and build our foundation upon, but two. It is vitally important for us as young adults to gain our own sense of authority in this world, to differentiate from the voices around us and learn to make decisions for ourselves. But for those of us who believe in Jesus, and have given our lives to him, our voice is not the only voice. We now have an extraordinary gift—we have the gift of good company within our very souls.

Scripture tells us that the Holy Spirit dwells in us. What this means, I have no idea. Does the Holy Spirit dwell in our cells? In our bodies? In our thoughts? I don't know. But I know it's true. Somehow, the Spirit is there, speaking inside of my heart as clearly as a thought, yet completely silent to the physical ear.

The key is learning to discern the Spirit's voice, and that's not something any of us can do on our own. In fact, I think it's dangerous to try. No, there needs to be a way to vet this internal dialogue that goes on between the Holy Spirit and one's internal voice.

I believe that whatever the Holy Spirit tells us will be confirmed around us, in Scripture, in the sermons we hear, and through other good company. Also, we should share what we feel the Holy Spirit is telling us with our church community, pastor, parents, and small group. They'll let us know if we're off track.

That was the incredible beauty of my relationship with Jackie. She was my sounding board, my mirror. I held up to her my every thought, emotion, and belief, and she reflected back to me what of my life was broken, and what the Holy Spirit was moving, breathing, and giving new life to. I began to learn to distinguish this voice out of time and space and the ways in which it conversed with my own internal voice. I found good company within my very soul.

12

DIFFERENTIATION

From the moment Nathan was conceived, he was separating, his cells splitting and growing. Some cells became tissue, some bone, some muscle. But all the while, he was one—the same. The DNA never changed.

Developmental biology calls this "differentiation." When a cell differentiates from another cell, it breaks away and evolves into a specialized cell. Each cell can be vastly different from the next, but they all come from the same source. So while a differentiated cell can have very different physical characteristics from the parent cell, it shares the same genome, the same code. It's telling that the title given between the differentiated cells is "adult" cell and "daughter" cell. We are for our whole lives, from the moment God breathes us into existence, constantly separating from home and then returning to it new, different, changed.

By the time my contractions started and I arrived on the heels of labor, I was changed. My first year in Bellingham with all its transition and loss and illness had pounded me thin, and yet, by the time I arrived at labor and delivery, I was beginning to heal. We had diagnosed my gluten sensitivity, and I had been taking my anti-anxiety medicine for nearly a month. The shattered glass in my gut had pieced itself together and disappeared, and the heavy despair that leaned in on me like an old companion had done the same. Though I was feeling raw and fragile, I was feeling much, much better than I had felt for months.

The morning of Nathan's birth, Dwayne and I scrubbed through the apartment, cleaning. Noelle was at Loving Space for her weekly school day, and Dwayne had taken the day off, since my contractions had gotten fairly close and regular. I had woken up at intervals in the night to the vise grip of early labor squeezing my abdomen, but nothing unbearable. "I could be doing this for days," I rehearsed to myself, imagining a week of similar contractions punctuating the minutes and hours. A veritable no-man's-land of expectations shadows every labor and delivery. Who of us can know how the story will go? Will our labors be slow and time consuming? Or will they be unimaginably quick? Will our babies be born with the bone-crushing pain of natural childbirth, or with the latex gloves and masks of epidurals and interventions? Will our babies be born complication-free? Or will we see them from behind the curtain of a cesarean section? Will they be born with the tiny wail and scream of life's first breath? Or will they be born with the purple blue silence of resuscitation? We can hope; we can wish; but we cannot know.

So, certain that this labor would be a long drawn-out tale, I got busy cleaning the apartment. "Dwayne could you mop the kitchen floor while I clean the bathroom?" I shouted from the bedroom, as I ran the duster over our dresser. I heard him opening and shutting doors in the other room, presumably getting out the mop and bucket. Soon I heard water pouring from the sink and knew he had heard me. We smiled at each other as we crossed paths, me stopping every few minutes pulled in like a fist around each contraction. They were beginning to leave me breathless, but still nothing that signaled I was on the verge of going to the hospital. "I could be doing this for days," I recited to myself and skirted around Dwayne to the cupboard above the kitchen sink where I kept my cleaning supplies. I opened the door, pulled down a rag and tile cleaner, and rounded the cabinet just as another massive rubber band tightened around the lower half of my body. I stopped mid-step, mid-breath, frozen in time.

Suddenly, what felt like a water balloon snapped and splashed to my feet in a massive puddle. Dwayne looked at me thunderstruck, knowing crossing his face. This exact thing had happened with Noelle.

"My water just broke!" I exclaimed. Immediately, he ran for the trash bag and towel for the passenger seat, my overnight bag, and we ran for the car. That was 10:30 in the morning. Just an hour and ten minutes later, I lay crumpled and elated on the hospital bed, with Nathan warm in my arms. I had not known how cold I was, wracked as I had been by the throes of labor, until the minute the nurses laid Nathan on me. I did not experience anything like it with Noelle (with her, I was numb from the waist down with an epidural), and I did not expect to experience it with him. "Oh my baby," was all I could utter in complete exhaustion as I felt him wriggling on my belly.

That is perhaps the closest moment I've had to being completely one with my son. He has been separating from me ever since, growing, learning, becoming more and more independent. He will be two years old in two days, and now he can go to sleep without me and eat without me. Now, if he is tired enough and wants me to snuggle him before bed, he will lay his head on my chest and hug my belly like we did on that first morning of his life. But I feel him differentiating from me every day in small ways now. One day, he will do this in much bigger ways.

In his book *Mentor*, Laurent Daloz talks about this necessity to leave, the almost biological compulsion we have to separate from where we began. The irony is that though we differentiate from our parents, we are still quite literally made of the same stuff as they are. And so the ultimate benefit of separating, splitting, dividing, is that we can turn around and see our DNA, our original code with new eyes. Daloz writes, "Our old life is still there, but its meaning has profoundly changed because we have left home, seen it from afar, and been transformed by that vision."[1] In other words, we turn around and look back on where we've come from and find the landscape glittering with lights and shadows we never saw before.

An old Japanese folktale tells the story of Momotaro and the Island of Ogres.[2] While reading this story the other night to Noelle, I couldn't help but think of this transformation of home, and the balancing act Baxter Magolda says that good company holds for us: autonomy and connectedness.[3] In the process of differentiating, we come to learn in what ways we are both deeply tied to the community around us, but also separate and other than them. Momotaro's journey from young man to adult reminds me of this delicate dance between two seemingly disparate poles: differentiating from our surroundings, yet holding them close.

Momotaro is a gift from the gods. He arrives bobbing and swirling on the eddies of a lake, in the shining orb of a pink and gold fruit. The peach-like orb floats to a barren woman, trying to do her laundry. She gathers the strange fruit up in her arms and carries it home to her husband, a woodcutter. Thinking that the orb is something to eat, they cook rice and prepare to feast. But when they slice open the strange gift, they find in its center a baby boy. (If only having babies were so painless and uncomplicated!)

Better than any food or riches, the couple rejoices over this gift of a child and raise the boy as their own. They name him "Momotaro," meaning "peach boy." And he is a *peach* of a boy. Supernaturally strong, wise as a sage, uncommonly good. He is a rising sun over the couple's humble home.

But in the shadows of their land lies a dark threat. Just off the coast stands an island of ogres—Onigashima. These ogres routinely pillage the mainland, carrying off food and treasures, and killing everyone in their path. As he gets older, Momotaro hears of the rascally ogres and decides that it is his life's mission to sail to Onigashima, vanquish the brutes, and return everything they've stolen to the rightful owners.

Then comes the scene that reminds me most of differentiation. He stands in his mother and father's doorway, their thin bamboo walls cutting clean, peaceful lines away from him.

"Mother, Father," he says. "I am so grateful for the love and care you have given me. But you must let me go away for a little while."

The couple look at him surprised. Tears fill his mother's eyes. His father looks away. Here before them stands their precious son, their gift from the gods, their peach boy. How can they possibly let him go?

I've talked to many parents during the last few years that I've been writing and researching about young adult development. Every few months, I run across a mother or father in their late forties or early fifties, and they ask me, "What are you writing about?"

"The shipwrecks we hit in our twenties," I tell them, and immediately their eyes light with recognition.

"I would love for my son to read that," a mother told me once, as we stood in the doorway of her office. From there her voice lowered and she began to share with me the story of her young adult son, out in the world battling depression and struggling to find his vocation.

A friend and former professor of mine told me, "The children who leave our home are making choices about where to go to graduate school, where to live, who to marry. These are such big decisions, and it doesn't always feel like they're ready to make these decisions. But there they are, out on the tight rope, without a net."

My heart breaks when I talk to these parents and I sense just how worried they are about their children. I've listened as parents confide in me how their young adults have left the faith behind, are struggling with mental illness, are struggling to find a vocation, or are marrying the wrong person.

Again this same professor friend said to me so poignantly, "I've never felt as powerless as I do now in my parenting experience."

In the face of such powerlessness, the woodcutter and his wife look at their son and realize they have really only one choice to make—to let him go. With his parents behind him and Onigashima before him, Momotaro sets out to face the demons within and without. But as these stories go, it is not long before Momotaro runs into a companion. This companion comes in the form of a spotted dog, who initially threatens to rip Momotaro to pieces for walking through his meadow without permission. But once he hears of Momotaro's noble quest, he howls, tucks his tail between his legs and begs for forgiveness.

"I've heard of your great strength from the other animals," the dog demurs in his scruffy voice. "Let me come with you, and I will do whatever I can to help you in your quest." And so the dog joins Momotaro, as does a feisty monkey and a pheasant with a brilliant plumage.

When Momotaro arrives at the shores of the island of ogres, he is not alone. He has with him three animals, each clever in their own right, and together the four of them conquer an entire city of savages. Momotaro returns home gilded with riches. Miraculously, there is enough treasure for the rightful owners, and extra for Momotaro and his traveling companions.

He builds an opulent home for his parents, and he and his family and his animal friends live in harmony ever after. But, as the folktale goes, as amazed as his parents are by the wealth, it is the safe return of their son, now transformed into the pillar of a man, that fills them with profound joy.

Momotaro had to split, separate, divide from his home, just as every cell in his divinely delivered body had done from the moment of his creation somewhere in the mist of the lake. And so must we. We must learn to become autonomous. The word *autonomous* comes from the ancient Greek for "self law." To be autonomous is to make our own laws, to govern ourselves, to be an independent country with our own currency, language, and culture. It is to be free.

And yet, this state of independence is a dangerous place to stand. All on our own, we can delude ourselves and split and fracture in the isolation. If we are to make this mythic transformation from young adult to adult, we must also understand our part in the whole. We need our traveling companions, who will help us take on a world that sometimes can feel more like Onigashima than like home. And when we return home, we find that it is still there, only now it is a part of us—deeper, wider than before. The riches we carry back have less to do with material wealth, and more to do with the ever expanding immensity of our own heart.

Just like Momotaro, Nathan will one day leave me. And long before that, he will be reminding me in big and small ways that he is no longer one with me, but different, separate, his own being.

In truth, giving birth to him was my own differentiation, my own defiant act of autonomy. No one else in that room could have given birth to him in the way I did, and yet, I could not have done it without Dwayne. I held with all my might, clinging to his shoulders, my face buried into the warmth of his neck. The poor man could hardly move, I had him in such a vise grip. But I knew somehow, that if I pulled my face away from his body, from the warmth of his skin, my resolve would dissolve.

Weeks before I lay in the hospital, Dwayne and I agreed that for this labor and delivery, we would hire a doula. I had heard from a friend that women who had doulas during their labors were less likely to experience postpartum depression. Unlike midwives, doulas are not licensed to deliver your baby. Instead, doulas are like physical trainers for labor. They support you through every step of the process, helping you find the best exercises and positions that allow labor to go smoothly. They help you prepare mentally for the coming trial, and they also liaison between you and the doctor, helping to explain to you what the doctor says and likewise helping to advocate on your behalf to the doctor.

Mary, our doula, swept into the room in her long skirt and took her place beside my bed. "I need an epidural!" I howled.

The nurses chattered away. "Honey, you're either going to have an epidural or a baby."

I peeked at Mary between contractions, every muscle in my body turning to stone. She could see the confusion written all over my face. Mary leaned in toward me and explained, "Nathan's almost ready to come out. By the time the epidural kicks in, you'll be holding your son."

Just then a wave of panic washed over me. I felt like I was drowning in pain. I saw Mary and Dwayne's faces from beneath water, and my body sunk away from them like an anchor to the deep abyss of unconsciousness below.

"Relax this muscle," I heard Mary's voice from a distance. She was stroking the muscles along my forearm. Her caress snapped me back into the hospital room. "Focus on that muscle," she said. "Now relax it."

The pain ebbed for a moment. Then suddenly, it was gone, and I could feel everything inside of me bear down.

"Don't push! Don't push!" the nurses barked at me.

"How do I not push?" I shrieked. There was no stopping my body from doing what it was doing. I pressed my face deep into Dwayne's neck and breathed in the smell of his skin. Mary leaned close coaching me in my ear.

"Roll over onto your back," the doctor instructed, and I froze. I looked over at her and blinked, unable to process what she had just told me. "Roll over so we can deliver him," the doctor repeated.

"I can't," I said. Up until that point, I had been laboring on my side, with my upper body propped against Dwayne's chest and shoulders. Now they wanted me to roll over. I felt it deep in the fibers of my body that if I rolled over, I would not be able to push out my son. Later, I would learn that some say delivering on your back is actually the least efficient way to give birth. It situates the baby in such a way that it is harder for the mother to push. In the moment, I could not have explained the biology and physics of all this, I just *knew* that if I rolled onto my back all the forward motion we had achieved until that moment would come to a screeching halt.

"Quickly," the doctor said, growing urgent. The nurses took my legs and began to try and rotate me onto my back.

I looked up at Mary, panic rising again like water. "I can't!" I choked. "I can't." Without having to explain to her any further, Mary nodded her head. She slipped away from the bed and spoke gently in the doctor's ear. The beauty of using Mary's services was that she had been working with these doctors for sixteen years, helping women deliver their babies. She carried a certain amount of credibility with the doctors that I did not. I watched as the doctor listened to her, nodded, and turned to the nurses.

"OK, she can deliver on her side."

This was a transitional moment in my experience of autonomy and connectedness. I knew with everything in my body what I needed in order to give birth to my baby in the healthiest, least complicated manner. No one could have told me this. I knew with all the certainty of a woman white-knuckling her way through a rite of passage. But even as I knew it, I could never have enacted this rite without connectedness, without Mary coaching me and advocating for me, without Dwayne standing beside my bed, firm and present as a deeply rooted tree.

This is the balance of autonomy and connectedness, the balance of being individual and yet also learning how to collaborate with those around us. This is what it means to be a fully realized adult:

We learn where others end and the core of our own being begins. We learn with growing strides of confidence what we believe and how we fit into the world, what we are capable of and what we can do, but this does not come at the expense of community, networks, and good company. Quite to the contrary. Good company helps us learn that we know better where we stand in life, because we learn with growing acuity with whom we are standing.

13

THE GUARDIANS
OF OUR PAST

"The medicine will get your biology back in order, but you will lose your mind again if you don't get out and get connected," the psychiatrist looked at me from across the coffee table. She was in her mid-fifties, an attractive woman with dark curly hair, light eyes, and big, expressive gestures. "You need to find an out-of-home office," her hands swept across the space in front of her body. "Do you have one of those?" I shook my head, trying to envision what she was talking about. "Do you have a coffee shop you go to, to work?" I shook my head again. "Well!" her hands punctuated the air and she smiled. "Go to Café Allegro! They have a toy area. Put the baby down, let him play while you check your e-mail and work. You need to get out of your apartment and get connected with the world again."

Dr. Carter was right. As I looked back over the past year, I saw clearly how our apartment on the second floor of Edens Hall had become my own personal prison. Due to pregnancy, sickness, and a lack of work, I had spent nearly every day alone with Noelle in the confines of those walls. Because of my sickness, I hadn't connected with any of the mothers at preschool or church, opting instead to lay on the couch in pain.

With those words of instruction from my psychiatrist, I set out to join the local MOPS (mothers of preschoolers) group, a community of mothers with young children that got together two Tuesdays a month at a megachurch on the outskirts of Bellingham. Easily over one hundred women congregated from the corners of Whatcom County for MOPS each month.

From the first moment I set foot in the large open space of the church foyer and fellowship hall, I felt my spirits rise. "Hello!" A cute woman with short brown hair and a button nose sidled up to me. "I'm Carrie, your discussion group leader! Our table is right over here." Noelle was safe and sound in the classroom dedicated to three- and four-year-olds, and I carried Nathan wrapped up in the ergo carrier close to my chest. He was just a few weeks old, small and pink, and full of my heart. At the table, I found a chair with my name on it, a craft ready for me to assemble, as well as a travel mug full of candy. "This is for you." Carrie scooted the travel mug toward me and turned to welcome the next weary mother joining our table.

Over the course of the next year, MOPS became a resort for me, a haven of free gifts, love, and support. It was like going to an emotional spa where my spirit, body, and mind were pampered month after month. Each meeting we learned more about parenting from new and interesting speakers such as the Super-Nanny of Whatcom County, or a self-defense expert who taught us how to help our kids defend themselves against bullying. During those early meetings when Nathan was so small, I barely held him. The mothers around my table whose children were out of arm's reach would carry Nathan the entire meeting, cooing over him and cuddling him. Going to MOPS felt like dipping into the ripples of a cold creek on an unbearably hot day. In the presence of these other lovely young mothers, I not only began to heal from a war-weary year, I also began to embrace my role as a parent in new and thoughtful ways.

Not that I was any less of a parent when it was just Noelle and me, but somehow, bringing Nathan into our family, along with me not working, allowed me to sink into my days as a mother in ways I hadn't done until that point. I woke up to my responsibilities with them and the power I had as a mother to shape and create their worlds. It was, and still is, a beautiful, sacred task. I spent more time reading and learning how to do science and art projects with the kids. We joined a gymnastics class for Noelle, where I was able to meet more mothers. I also signed us up for a Music Together class, which Noelle and Nathan both loved. Here, too, I began to connect with other parents in the community. I felt the tendrils of my identity leafing and growing up a new trellis of friendship and community.

During this season, Dwayne and I discovered Dr. Charles Fay's book *Love and Logic: Magic for Early Childhood*, which revolutionized the way we were parenting Noelle.[1] While the twos hadn't been all that terrible, Noelle's threes were nearly unbearable. She lashed out in vicious and terrifying ways, scratching and kicking and biting me. More than once she drew blood. I stood in church one day, tears streaming down my face as I thought about my precious girl and the quandary of her behavior. I felt helpless and devastated. Little by little, Dr. Fay, along with the advice of other mothers, helped us learn how to negotiate the turbulent waters of Noelle's tantrums.

In those days, I felt able to embody and embrace my identity as a parent with a new sense of fullness, a fullness that has continued to this day. And as I've identified more and more with my role as a mother and parent, a question has dogged me: Is it possible for parents to be good company as we watch our children grow into the young adult years? This question perplexes me primarily because our parents inherently represent the home we need to separate from in order to see ourselves through new eyes. And also because they are perhaps the most emotionally invested in our self-authorship journey.

The answer is years away for me, since Noelle and Nathan are so young, but still I see parent after parent around me struggling to know how to help their young adult children. I think it's incredibly difficult for our parents to watch us struggle with huge life decisions, and not want to step in and try and protect us from the pain of shipwreck. But this urge to protect runs counterintuitive to the organic process of learning that happens for us as young adults.

I decided to ask a friend of mine who is a pastor's wife and the mother of five young adults. For many reasons, I've chosen to keep her anonymous. So we'll just call her Hester for now. Hester is perhaps one of the loveliest women I have ever met. She is a deeply thoughtful, reflective, sweet-spirited woman with a steady twinge of self-doubt. I deeply admire Hester and wanted to learn from her how to be a parent of young adults. Unfortunately, Hester has been watching in agony for the last few years as her son, born and raised in the church, has been making a steady fade from faith. I wanted to find out from Hester if she felt it was possible to be good company to her son.

She first shared with me the depths of despair she has sunk to watching her son go through his faith shipwreck. "I think, it is *very difficult* for parents to be 'learning partners' — especially when you see your adult child intentionally walking away from Jesus. It breaks your heart! Everything in you wants to try to convince them that they are headed for a cliff."

She asked me, "Is it any easier for parents who watch their child shipwreck in other areas? All I know is that the faith shipwreck has been very hard on me and my husband. The verse from 3 John has always been the cry of my own heart for my kids while they were growing up: 'I have no greater joy than to hear that my children are walking in the truth' [v. 4]. There is *nothing* I want more for them than a vibrant, passionate relationship with Jesus on their own. No money or fame is more important to me. Satan knows this and has attacked me in my most vulnerable spot—my own child and his relationship with Jesus."

You can hear the anguish in Hester's voice through her words. It washes over me even now as I read her thoughts in black and white. There is nothing black and white about watching her child leave behind the church, faith, and a relationship with Jesus. At the risk of sounding melodramatic, it seems to be something like watching your child die, and feeling totally helpless to rescue him or her.

This may sound absurd, that our parents may feel the same kind as grief of a parent of a child who has died, but listening to Hester makes me feel that perhaps this comparison isn't so far off. After all, those of us raised in the church, and those who have read James Fowler's stages of faith development, understand that faith touches the core of our being and our entire identity in a way that other identities don't.

As William Cantwell-Smith says,

Faith, then, is a quality of human living. At its best it has taken the form of serenity and courage and loyalty and service: a quiet confidence and a joy which enable one to feel at home in the universe, and to find meaning in the world and in one's own life, a meaning that is profound and ultimate, and is stable no matter what may happen to oneself at the level of immediate event. Men and women of this kind of faith face catastrophe and confusion, affluence and sorrow, unperturbed; face opportunity with conviction and drive; and face others with cheerful charity.[2]

That final line strikes me as particularly significant: Those of us who live by faith are able to meet pain and suffering, joy and success . . . untroubled. It reminds me of Paul's declaration, "I know what it is to be in need, and I know what it is to have plenty. I have learned the secret of being content in any and every situation, whether well fed or hungry, whether living in plenty or in want. I can do all this through him who gives me strength" (Phil. 4:12–13). We can face life unworried because we are anchored by a relationship with the transcendent, a relationship which we as Christians acknowledge is made possible through Jesus Christ.

So when Hester watches her son walk away from his faith, it strikes me that she's not just watching him leave behind a set of beliefs. Hester believes she is watching her son walk away from the essence of life itself.

It may be hard for those of us who are beginning to think critically about our family, home, and growing-up years, to understand why our movement away from our parents' beliefs crushes them. But I think we have to understand that they are so emotionally invested in our journey that it's hard for them to step back and see our shipwreck process for what it is—a crucial stage of development.

And that is precisely why I wonder if parents can be good company.

I asked Hester if she felt like she could offer the kind of challenge and support to her son that good company is defined by, and in essence she said, "No."

"In my opinion, I think my role as a mother is slightly different. I do support him in whatever way I can. I don't, however, feel it's my place to challenge him, because he is not asking for help from me or his dad—and he does not want us to tell him what to do. At first when we tried, he shut us down." I think Hester's son isn't ready for them yet, because he thinks he knows what they're going to say. He's lived with them for twenty years and has internalized their faith as well as their beliefs on everything from politics to their taste in movies.

So perhaps, here's the hurdle to parents being good company: It's not just that they're so close to us that it's hard for them to offer us the kind of space we need to struggle and grow, but it might also be because *we* are too close to them to allow them the space to speak into our journeys.

With that in mind, I don't think it's impossible for parents to be good learning partners. Take for example my friend Brooke. She's on the cusp of graduating from Western Washington University with a major in photojournalism. The woman looks as if she's just walked out of the forest, with strawberry blond hair, freckles, and green eyes that dance like sunlight on leaves. When

I asked her who her good company is, she listed her mom as number one on the list. She said, "My mom has been great company because I feel like I can call her at any time, and she is able to talk to me and give me advice. We share laughter and a history that cannot be replaced. At the same time, I am able to give her advice too, so it is an equitable relationship. Unconditional love also exists in our relationship."

The key word there, I think, is *equitable*. Brooke's mom is able to be good company to her daughter because somewhere along the way the power differential shifted. From Brooke's explanation, it sounds like she feels on equal footing with her mother and free to speak into her mother's life as much as her mother speaks into hers. It sounds like they relate in Brooke's young adult years more as friends.

But whether or not we all feel we can have that type of friendship relationship with our parents, I do think there are things parents can do to walk with us through these rocky young adult years. And Hester has discovered these things completely on her own.

Hester told me that she realized she could not challenge her son, because he wasn't asking for help from her or her husband. Instead, she dropped her agenda and let her son lead the way. "Now, because we are not pushing our agenda on him, he is more open to dialogue—but he has to be the one to say that he wants to talk about a certain subject. We allow him to talk about it if he brings it up, but we have learned to just nod and keep our comments to ourselves. He is not ready for us yet."

Hester is learning how to hold the space for her son to explore and learn on his own, while simultaneously learning to hold her anxiety in check. She still worries, but she's able to separate that anxiety from her interactions with her son. Hester has managed to learn to step back. As much as her son's turn from faith kills her on the inside, she still loves him, and loves him enough to put her own personal pain on hold in order to better journey with her son through his shipwreck. "Eventually, I had to distance myself from my son . . . in a healthy way, to set some boundaries. I had to release—actually relinquish—him to the Lord daily. Many times daily!" And ultimately, this distance is what is saving their relationship. It is what is even giving her a place on the journey with her son. Her ability to withhold advice but still be present is what has earned back her son's trust and allowed him to crack the door open again to her.

He has now begun to ask her out to lunch on a regular basis. Hester cherishes these moments and is careful to put into practice the principles she feels she's learning during this season of influencing a young adult.

Through her personal prayer times, Hester has felt like the Lord has given her some very tangible ways to relate to her son. She listed them out for me, and I share them with you here, because perhaps we can share them with our parents and help them see what they can do to be good learning partners for us. She said the Lord had directed her to approach her son in these ways: First, she must be loving toward him and wait for him like the father waited for his son to return home. (See Mark 15:11–32 for the whole story.)

Whether or not our parents are Christians, we might explain to them that what we are going through is normal, it's developmental, and it's not our final destination; it's simply our journey to a stronger sense of self. It may feel to them, as they watch us up-close, that the questions we are asking and that the decisions we are making are the end of the story, but what Hester touches on here with this story of her son is that where her son is struggling today is not where he will end up for the rest of his life.

We might try and help our parents see that we are all on our way back around, back to a sense of self that is deeper and more nuanced than what it was before. Our political beliefs or faith may be slightly different from our parents', but we will probably not abandon those beliefs forever. This is just a part of owning them for ourselves.

Second, Hester decided she needed to put a muzzle on her lips. She told me that, "The Lord made it very clear that I didn't need to talk to my son about my concerns for him, but instead, to talk to the Lord about it—as much as I needed." Hester has found a great way to manage her anxiety about her son by praying. It can be so easy for our parents to manage their anxiety by trying to manage us, but that ultimately is a misguided attempt, because in the end it only manages to alienate them from us, and drive us away. Better instead for them to take their anxiety to the One who sees the beginning and end of our story. Again, if our parents are not Christians, perhaps they could take their worry to another parent of a young adult.

Third, after talking to me, Hester decided she needed to ask the Lord to bring good learning partners alongside her son. Now, she didn't use the term *learning partners*, that's Baxter Magolda's phrase. Hester used the term *godly people*, which I believe is also valuable in its own right as we are working through our faith questions, but in terms of shipwrecks that touch every aspect of our journey, I think it's helpful for our parents to pray for us to find good learning partners who can help us discover these other areas of our identity, including faith.

Fourth, Hester also felt very strongly that the Lord told her not to cry or act worried about her son when he was around.

Instead, she felt she was to be confident and joyful when he was around.

I find this exquisitely insightful. Ultimately, if our parents want to be a part of our journey, we are so much more likely to include them on the ride if they are happy and easy to be around. It only defeats us when every time we are at our parents' house they are fussing and crying over us. That's exhausting and also leaves us with very few answers. It doesn't help us figure things out any better if we now have to carry the weight of our parents' anxiety as well as our own. If they are walking with us in peace and joy, even if it is temporary joy that disintegrates the moment we're not around, it allows us the safe space we need to work through our own internal dissonance.

I love Hester's realizations, because she's an example to me of how a parent can walk that very difficult tightrope of parent-hood, and yet also being some measure of good company. We absolutely need our parents along on this ride. We need their unconditional love and support. We need them because they are the guardians of our past, our history, they know us better than anyone else. However, as Hester helps us see, they may have a unique role to play in our shipwreck that is supplemental to the role of being good company.

14

THRIVE

I set Nathan, just four weeks old, on the blanket. Behind me
Lake Padden rippled quietly beneath the summer sun, and in
front of me the playground rippled with the energy of children
climbing, running, and squealing. Today was my first day at
home with both the kids alone. Mom and Dad had come and
gone, as had my sister. All of them spread the ointment of their
love and care over those first burning newborn days. Soon
it was time for Dwayne to go back to work, and here I was at
the park. I had successfully scheduled a play date with a new
friend, Liz, and had managed to get myself and both the kids
loaded into the car with all our snacks, diapers, sippy cups, and

sunscreen. Now, I was ready for a nap, and it was only ten in the morning.

Liz sat on the blanket in front of me, her heart-shaped face framed by a crop of brown waves. She wore shining aviator sunglasses that hid her large, quiet brown eyes. "Do you need some help?" she offered as I settled onto the blanket to unclip the carrier that held Nathan. I shook my head and leaned back to check on Noelle, who was busy scampering up a ladder onto the play set.

"How are you doing?" Liz asked in her liquid voice. She had a wonderful way of pausing before she spoke, even between sentences, as if she were carefully piecing together her thoughts. Just listening to her easy pace unraveled the knot in my chest ever so slightly.

"Oh, OK," I said, and then unexpectedly, I felt the prick of tears. I pushed my sunglasses close to my face immediately embarrassed. I had only known Liz a little more than a month and certainly did not feel ready to start crying in front of her.

I met Liz about two weeks before Nathan was born at the Chuckanut Writers Conference. I sat on a low cement wall on the campus of Whatcom Community College, an attractive campus situated on the other side of Bellingham. It was a clear June day, by Bellingham standards, and the sun shone bright and white in that diamond way that it does so far from the equator. The morning was beautiful but not nearly warm enough for me. People scattered around the courtyard like coins in a wishing well. We each wore a lanyard with our name and city of origin. In just forty-eight hours, we would be calling each other by first names, laughing and eating together, and exchanging phone numbers. For now, we were still strangers.

I glanced to my left and saw a woman about the same age as me sitting a little way down the wall. This was Liz. I was drawn to her open, thoughtful expression. Whether it was the Holy Spirit prompting my heart to talk to her or the vibe coming from her general direction—I think a bit of both—I felt certain that I would talk to her and that she would be easy company.

I leaned toward her, situating my pregnant belly so as not to have it interfere with my introduction. "Hi!" I said, breaking the stillness between us. She turned, slightly taken aback that a stranger was addressing her. "I'm Christin," I said, and she smiled. By the end of the day, I felt certain that if Liz liked me half as much as I liked her, we were going to be more than easy company for each other; we would be friends.

After the conference, Liz invited me to join her writing group, and I was so excited by the invitation, I just about jumped into her lap. We exchanged phone numbers and agreed to do play dates with our girls every once in a while. Hence our morning on the blanket at Lake Padden Park, watching as our girls circled away from us to play, then back toward us for snacks and drinks.

"I just get so overwhelmed," I said haltingly, "when I think about what it's going to be like without Dwayne to help." I decided to stop talking at that point, because I could feel the fissure in my composure splitting.

Liz folded her legs under her and turned toward me. She moved her glasses off her face and onto her mop of curls. "I find . . . that it's better not to look at the big picture . . . all at once . . . but rather to just take each day . . . moment by moment." The fissure stopped its threatening fracture. I looked at her kind face, and then down to see Nathan sleeping soundly on the blanket.

"Yes," I thought. "I just need to take each day segment by segment, even five minutes by five minutes." The weight lifted from my chest just a bit.

Segment by segment, I pressed out into my second year in Bellingham. And little by little, I found myself not just living, but flourishing. If the first year had been a slog through depression, isolation, pain, and grief, the second year was a year of nourishment, joy, and deep contentment. To the writing group, we added

Amy, a ballet teacher who was also an exquisite writer. Amy, Liz, and I went to poetry nights in Bellingham and read our poems. We shared our first drafts and deepest secrets with one another. We watched as our girls laughed and roared and played together. The combination of MOPS, my small group at church, the writing group with Amy and Liz, as well as the numerous other mothers I met through preschool became a symphony of music that sang me through my second year in Bellingham.

Moment after moment during that second year, I lifted my head from the bustle of childcare and writing and thought to myself, "I am thriving." Jackie's word had indeed come true. But I wasn't thriving because of an absence of pain or loss or struggle. In truth, it had been the pain and struggle that had pushed the fractures in my being to the surface, and forced me to pay attention to things I would have continued ignoring.

For example, though I had never thought I had a gluten sensitivity before getting pregnant, I couldn't deny that I felt so much better now that I had cut it out of my diet. Not only was the pain gone, it seemed to me that my skin was clearing up, my energy was up, and so were my spirits. Because of the pain and stress of my sickness, Dwayne and I had started going to counseling for our marriage, recognizing that neither one of us knew how to cope very well together, or even on our own, with chronic pain. My pain brought out the worst in me and the anxiety in Dwayne—an ugly combination. But as a result, during our time in counseling, our marriage also began to thrive in new and beautiful ways. I was also thriving as a mother, connected as I was to an abundance of resources and support, not just through MOPS, but through the mothers at preschool. I had also finished writing my first book, *Shipwrecked in L.A.*, five weeks before Nathan was born in July 2011, and was eventually able to sell it six months later over Christmas.

I held Jackie's word close to my heart and whispered a regular prayer of gratitude. "Thank you," I hummed. "Thank you for never letting go. Thank you for staying close."

15

RELEVÉ, SOUS-SOUS, AND BALANCE

I stood awkwardly at the bar—not a pub or a place you go for a drink, but a literal, metal bar, cold and sturdy at my waist. The young body in front of me could not have been more than seventeen, and she looked so sure in her limbs, so elegant in her pink tights, black leotard, and flesh-colored ballet shoes. I stood there in the only things I could find to wear to a ballet class: black leggings, a bright teal, lacy tank top, and socks. I had not been working out much that year, or let's be honest, the thirty years before that, and didn't have much of any kind of active wear in my closet.

As part of my plan to connect to the world around me, get out of the apartment, and stay mentally, emotionally, and physically healthy (just as my psychiatrist had instructed), I joined a ballet class in downtown Bellingham. The class started at 7 p.m., perfect timing for a young mom. The kids were bathed and ready for bed before I left. I made sure to nurse Nathan and hand him off to Dwayne for bedtime, just as I swung out the door to my first ballet class.

I would have liked to have died standing in the studio, painfully self-conscious. "What am I doing here?" I screamed internally. The idea had seemed so wonderful before I actually showed up, even though I had never taken a single ballet class in my entire life. Here I was in a room full of teenagers and adults who had all clearly had years of practice.

My friend and ballet teacher, Amy, spotted me from the front of the room and waved vigorously. I hunched over and waved sheepishly back. My eyes skirted the room, taking in all the lovely shapes and sizes of bodies around me, all uniform in their tight black leotards. Just beyond the string of mirrors on the right hand wall, I eyed the door and tried to figure out how to best make an early exit.

"Don't worry," a young man took his place at the bar behind me. "It's hard at first, but you'll get it. It just takes practice." He smiled kindly, and I nodded, voiceless. For those first few weeks of class, I was certain that every eye was on me as I jutted my legs out at wrong angles and stumbled my way through the warm-up routines.

"Let's start with a demi plié two times with arm a la seconde, one grande plié arm ending en haut," Amy stood at the front of the room, tall and fair, curly blond hair, and light eyes. She had apple cheeks and a loud, raucous laugh, one that catches you off guard and swings you up high in the air. "Sorry, messed that up!" she laughed as she switched her weight and struck a different pose. "Let's make it a relevé for two counts, lower, cambre forward, recover, tendu to second. Repeat with stretch to barre in second, away from barre in fourth, and cambre back in fifth. Relevé, sous-sous, and balance."

And with that, the class launched into a routine as alien to me as sign language. Still, in moments of abandon, I would get lost in the movements, the feel of my arms and legs and torso stretching in such fluid ways. I had moments when the self-consciousness would melt away, when I would remember a pose all on my own, and suddenly, easily, I would feel beautiful while doing ballet. Whether I looked it, is another matter. It was enough to watch Amy up close, to see the tiny flourish of fingers and toes that elevated each movement to the sublime, and to imagine that I was accomplishing the same.

Having danced since age three, Amy could leap and balance and almost float in ways that astounded me. Since taking Amy's ballet class, I have come to the opinion that something is lost when watching ballet from a distance on a stage. There are so many little moments in between the moves, the lifts, the spins, the leaps that are themselves quiet and perfect. These were the steps and half-turns, and tiny slips of limbs that escaped me during the entirety of my time in Amy's class, but I didn't stop trying. The young man's words echoed in my ears, "At first it's hard, but you'll get it."

I certainly have felt this way about being good company. I have repeatedly found myself listening to friends share with me, only to find my mind racing ahead wondering, "What am I supposed to say? What's the right way to respond? How do I make sure I help the most?" The answers have eluded me, and I've felt awkward and clunky, leaving long silent stretches when I should have spoken, or doling out heavy-handed advice that only crushed the conversation—but this was not for any lack of caring or wanting to help. I simply wasn't sure of the practiced in-between steps that would have led me to be a more confident learning partner.

We may be surrounded by wonderful people who can help us, but they may not be savvy in "good company" language or technique. If this is the case, and we have someone in our lives we think could be excellent company, but who perhaps needs a little coaching of their own on how to help, here are some suggestions about what we can tell our good company we need from them:

- I need you to respect my thoughts and feelings. I need you to acknowledge that I have something valuable to contribute, and I need you to trust that I am smart enough and thoughtful enough to work this out on my own, even if I make mistakes along the way.
- I need a place to process my thinking. You can support me by helping me work through the complex issues in my life. Talk it through with me; let me air out my thoughts. Sometimes, I just need to know I can bring my confusion and worry to you without feeling that you are going to judge what I'm telling you.
- I want to learn to face my problems myself. I want to be able to share the problems I'm having with you, but I don't necessarily want you to fix those problems, even if you have the power to. It's important for me to develop the personal authority to face these problems and learn how to address them without being rescued.
- I welcome your insights and questions, but not your advice. In other words, I would love to hear how you see my predicament, and I would love for you to ask me questions,

because that helps me see it from a new place, and that helps me learn how to be connected to the people around me in order to solve problems, but I don't necessarily need you to tell me what to do. Just give me your assessment, ask me questions that make me think, and let me make the decision for myself.

- I'm not giving up the front seat of my life. I'm still in charge here, mistakes and all. I don't need answers, and I don't need to be rescued, but I would love to have your company on this crazy ride.

These are the sort of elegant transitions between the listening and the caring that helps our good company best pull us together. At first it's hard to really grasp these points and put them to use, but with practice, time, and the motion of trying them over and over, good company can pirouette us into the dance of young adulthood.

16

GETTYSBURG, PENNSYLVANIA

"What do you think of moving to Gettysburg, Pennsylvania?" Dwayne asked, looking up at me over his computer.

"What?" I stopped, Nathan perched on my hip. The winter sun was fading into a slow spring, unwilling or unable to keep its cheery head above the horizon much past four o'clock in the afternoon. Dwayne, the kids, and I putzed around the apartment in a usual after-dinner buzz, trying to find things to do to keep busy inside, while outside the day grew dark. "I thought you didn't want to live east of the 5 freeway?" I half grinned. I was sort of teasing him, but also a little wary of a cross-country move. Things had finally started clicking together in Bellingham for me. I was finally thriving, and the thought of uprooting and starting all over again sent a quiet chill down my back.

"They use Marcia Baxter Magolda's residential education model like we do here at Western," he stopped to read my face. When he didn't get the look of excitement he was waiting for, he added, "And they provide a house."

I nearly dropped Nathan. The chill in my back dissolved as I looked around the second-floor apartment that had seen so much change, agony, and healing in the last two years. It was clean and simple and fine, but I felt my heart push out with longing. Imagine having a yard for the kids to play in. It almost made leaving my friends behind worth it. "OK," I said. "Tell me about Gettysburg."

After working for two years as a resident director at Western, Dwayne knew it was time for him to move up the proverbial ladder. Resident directors, after all, tend to be right out of graduate school in their mid-twenties. Not many come to the field married with kids. So when the job as an assistant director of residence life at a small liberal arts school in south central Pennsylvania opened up, he did some research.

As much as we loved Bellingham, there were no other residential colleges or universities close by where he might commute to a new job, so that the kids and I could continue our lives in Bellingham. Even a move to Seattle or across the not-so-distant border of Canada to Vancouver, would have meant a complete upheaval for our family. So when all was said and done, a move to Gettysburg didn't seem all that out of the question. Also, the allure of family within a couple hours drive from south central Pennsylvania, tipped my heart ever so slightly east. We had loved living on the West Coast for the last decade, seven years in L.A. and two years in Bellingham, but perhaps the tides were shifting again.

Over the next couple of weeks, Dwayne and I talked often about Gettysburg, trying to feel our way into a decision. The first was to decide whether or not we wanted Dwayne to apply for the job, thereby opening a route away from the West Coast for our family.

"What are you thinking about it?" I asked him one evening after dinner. I could see he was chewing on the idea of leaving.

"I think I could easily stay here another couple years, but then I wonder how much longer you and the kids could live here in the apartment."

"I think I could do it for another year," I answered, "but probably not beyond that." I turned and started scraping leftovers into a covered dish. "But I don't want the house to be the only reason why you take the job. What are you thinking about the work you might do there?" Dwayne and I talked into the evening, hashing out the possible transition. Neither one of us wanted him to apply for a job that we wouldn't be willing to accept.

Goodness knows, he and I had spent enough time arguing over things that simultaneously pricked our anxiety, but this particular topic of conversation energized us. We were able to have good-company conversations with one another about this significant life change, pushing each other to think it through and wrestle with the possible pitfalls and benefits.

As I think over how Dwayne and I have learned to conduct good-company conversations over the past few years, I would offer these bits of advice, not just from me, but from Marcia Baxter Magolda, and all those I learned from during my time at Western, too.

BE GENUINE

Part of being good company is knowing what we can realistically offer someone. "If you're not in a space to be good company, then don't be it," Dwayne's coworker and our family friend Stephanie told me once. I think that is brilliant advice. It takes a certain amount of self-awareness to recognize when we can help someone and when we can't.

I have been a sucker for overextending myself time and time again, because I felt that because I could recognize someone's need meant that I was therefore responsible to fill that need. It took me one frank session with my spiritual director, Jackie, to learn this wasn't necessarily true. When I came to her with a particular friendship that was marking my days with anxiety, she looked at me and asked, "Did you ask God if he wanted you to take on this particular ministry?" I blinked, dumbstruck. It had never occurred to me that a friendship could be a ministry, or furthermore, that I should even ask God if I should take on a friendship. It seemed to me that friendship was a gift and you don't decide whether or not you're going to accept a gift.

In retrospect, I saw how that particular friendship had hit me at just the wrong time. Because of life circumstances, I was struggling greatly with stress and anxiety. I wasn't in a healthy place to walk with another friend who was also so full of anxiety.

"It's not unkind or even unchristian to say to someone, 'I'm sorry, but I can't be your friend right now,'" Jackie shared with me, her eyes lighting on my heart. "It may be disappointing for them, if they want to be your friend, but it's not unkind."

This kind of honesty can feel difficult. After all, we don't want to hurt people's feelings or dismiss them. But if we force ourselves to try and offer support to someone when we don't have enough support of our own, we only hurt ourselves and them in the process.

Ultimately, being honest with ourselves and with the person who needs good company, pushes our friend to take ownership of their situation and go find the help that he or she needs.

LISTEN

Once you've established if you're in a good place to even be good company, the next step is simply to listen. As our friends tell us what they are struggling with, we can say things like, "That's really rough," or "Wow, I can see how this is draining you right now," or "Man, that's a heavy load to carry."

Statements like this work for two reasons: (1) They make us slow down and listen first, before we speak; and (2) they make our partners feel heard and signals that we're not going to try and fix this for them. As Baxter Magolda puts it, it's our job to "draw out their thinking and listen carefully rather than offering advice."[1] So we let them talk; we nod; we acknowledge what our partners are experiencing and what they are saying.

ASK QUESTIONS

After we've listened to our partners and heard what they're going through, the next thing we can do is ask questions that dig deep, that open the door for them to think about their experiences in new ways. Such as: So, have you thought about this?

What's going on in your head? Are you feeling torn up? Are you upset? What are your thoughts? What are your emotions? What's going on? These types of questions encourage our partners to start to step outside of their heads and get new perspective. Often just this act in and of itself suddenly makes their way forward clear. But if not, we can help them further by digging deeper.

Ultimately what we are trying to do is help our company organize their thoughts. Baxter Magolda writes that we should "help them reflect on and organize their ideas to come up with workable solutions."[2] So while we shouldn't try and give them advice or try and fix the problem for them, we can do one better — we can help them clarify the situation. This is so much more helpful, because it keeps the axis of control in their hands, not ours. By doing this, we can help clear out the cobwebs, clutter, and anxiety that could be clouding the answer.

REMIND YOURSELF TO STAY IN THE BACKGROUND

As hard as it is, we have to remember that we can't make our partners do anything, and that it's OK if they don't take our advice. This may even be heartbreaking, but we have to learn to let go.

Dwayne and I each had a vested interest in what the other decided about moving to Gettysburg, but we knew enough not to tell each other what to do. One by one, as we talked, the reasons why we were open to moving to Pennsylvania revealed themselves: We would be closer to family; we would be living in a house; Dwayne would be able to take on more responsibility in his job; and he would be able to work more regular hours.

"OK," I told Dwayne finally. "I'm willing to go."

And so, on a cool day in spring, Dwayne sent his application to a small but prestigious school on the East Coast.

THE OCEAN BEYOND

In the weeks leading up to our move, friend after friend stopped by the apartment to help me pack. Liz wrapped my dishes in newspaper and worked them into the empty spaces of a large brown box. Amy helped me clear out Noelle and Nathan's room, sorting what should be donated and what should be hauled across the country. Friends from our small group cooked us dinners and fed us when the kitchen was packed up. For the second time in two years, we loaded all of our earthly possessions into a small U-haul trailer, only this time the ride included one more child. For the second time in two years, I felt the air squeeze out of my lungs as I thought about leaving behind the beautiful friends who had held and taught me during our two years in the Pacific Northwest.

"But you are not arriving at Gettysburg the same woman you were when you arrived in Bellingham," my psychiatrist reassured me during our last meeting together. That was true. I knew better now what I needed in order to thrive. I had already researched the moms' group in Adams County, where we would be living. I already had found the gymnastics camp I was going to send Noelle to upon arrival. I had also, miraculously, landed an adjunct teaching job in the English department at the school where Dwayne would be working. Two weeks before we left Bellingham, I got a call from the head of the department, "We got your CV," she chirped. "Can you teach two classes this fall?"

Life was already falling into place for me in this new home in ways that it hadn't before we had arrived in Bellingham. But in addition to all this, I was arriving in Gettysburg a woman enlightened in finding the good company I would need to thrive in our new home and also being good company for the people who would cross my path. While the voyage ahead was, and always will be, unpredictable, there were some things now I had a measure of control over. The journey did not need to be without a crew. With that assurance in mind, I fastened the kids into their car seats, clicked my own seat belt, and watched as Bellingham

slipped behind the layers of green leafy hills and trees. Somewhere in that lush, vibrant foliage, I knew the bay stretched on,
out past the San Juan Islands, and then to the wide expanse of the
Pacific Ocean.

NOTES

INTRODUCTION

1. Sharon Daloz Parks, *Big Questions, Worthy Dreams: Mentoring Emerging Adults in Their Search for Meaning, Purpose, and Faith*, rev. ed. (San Francisco: Jossey-Bass, 2011), 39.

2. C. S. Lewis, *The Lion, the Witch and the Wardrobe*, The Chronicles of Narnia (New York: HarperTrophy, 1978), 80.

3. Marcia Baxter Magolda, *Authoring Your Life: Developing an Internal Voice to Navigate Life's Challenges* (Sterling, VA: Stylus, 2009), 1.

CHAPTER 1

1. C. G. Jung, *Psyche and Symbol: A Selection from the Writings of C. G. Jung*, ed. Violet S. de Laszlo (Garden City, NY: Doubleday, 1958), 77.

2. Ibid.

CHAPTER 2

1. Timothy Fry, ed., *The Rule of St. Benedict* (Collegeville, MN: The Liturgical Press, 1981), 257, 259.

2. Margaret Guenther, *Holy Listening: The Art of Spiritual Direction* (Cambridge, MA: Cowley, 1992), 9.

CHAPTER 3

1. Laurent Daloz, *Mentor: Guiding the Journey of Adult Learners* (San Francisco: Jossey-Bass, 1999), 27.

2. Nevitt Sanford, *Self and Society: Social Change and Individual Development* (New York: Atherton, 1966), 46.

CHAPTER 5

1. Marcia Baxter Magolda and Patricia M. King, eds., *Learning Partnerships: Theory and Models of Practice to Educate for Self-Authorship* (Sterling, VA: Stylus, 2004), 41.

2. John Purdie, telephone interview with author, summer 2013.

3. Ibid.

4. Ibid.

CHAPTER 6

1. John Purdie, telephone interview with author, summer 2013.

2. Marcia Baxter Magolda and Patricia M. King, eds., *Learning Partnerships: Theory and Models of Practice to Educate for Self-Authorship* (Sterling, VA: Stylus, 2004), 42.

CHAPTER 7

1. Marcia Baxter Magolda and Patricia M. King, eds., *Learning Partnerships: Theory and Models of Practice to Educate for Self-Authorship* (Sterling, VA: Stylus, 2004), 42.

2. Marcia Baxter Magolda, *Making Their Own Way: Narratives for Transforming Higher Education to Promote Self-Discovery* (Sterling, VA: Stylus, 2001), 195–196.

CHAPTER 8

1. Marcia Baxter Magolda and Patricia M. King, eds., *Learning Partnerships: Theory and Models of Practice to Educate for Self-Authorship* (Sterling, VA: Stylus, 2004), 42.

2. John Purdie, telephone interview with author, summer 2013.

CHAPTER 9

1. Marcia Baxter Magolda and Patricia M. King, eds., *Learning Partnerships: Theory and Models of Practice to Educate for Self-Authorship* (Sterling, VA: Stylus, 2004), 42.

2. "Principles of Good Practice for Student Affairs," accessed September 24, 2013, http://acpa.nche.edu/pgp/principle.htm.

CHAPTER 10

1. Gwen Jackson, personal communication with author, spring 2011.

2. Marcia Baxter Magolda and Patricia M. King, eds., *Learning Partnerships: Theory and Models of Practice to Educate for Self-Authorship* (Sterling, VA: Stylus, 2004), 43.

CHAPTER 11

1. Margaret Guenther, *Holy Listening: The Art of Spiritual Direction* (Cambridge, MA: Cowley, 1992), 32.

2. Ibid., 3.

3. Ibid., 27.

4. Ibid., 34.

5. Ibid., 39.

6. Marcia Baxter Magolda, *Authoring Your Life: Developing an Internal Voice to Navigate Life's Challenges* (Sterling, VA: Stylus, 2009), 11.

CHAPTER 12

1. Laurent Daloz, *Mentor: Guiding the Journey of Adult Learners* (San Francisco: Jossey-Bass, 1999), 27.

2. Stephanie Wada and Kano Naganobu. *Momotaro and the Island of Ogres* (New York: George Braziller, Inc., 2005).

3. Marcia Baxter Magolda and Patricia M. King, eds., *Learning Partnerships: Theory and Models of Practice to Educate for Self-Authorship* (Sterling, VA: Stylus, 2004), 37.

CHAPTER 13

1. Jim Fay and Charles Fay, *Love and Logic: Magic for Early Childhood* (Golden, CO: Love and Logic, 2000).

2. William Cantwell-Smith, *Faith and Belief*, quoted in James Fowler, *Stages of Faith: The Psychology of Human Development and the Quest for Meaning* (San Francisco: Harper & Row, 1981), 11.

CHAPTER 16

1. Marcia Baxter Magolda, *Authoring Your Life: Developing an Internal Voice to Navigate Life's Challenges* (Sterling, VA: Stylus, 2009), 15.

2. Ibid.

Finding Hope and Purpose When Your Dreams Crash

Most young adults encounter at least one "shipwreck" during their twenties. Everything you think you know about yourself, your life, your future, and even your faith suddenly breaks apart. You're left scrambling to construct a lifeboat that will take you back to the shore.

Christin Taylor knew how her life was going to turn out. She was going to be a missionary to the Hollywood film industry. But just eight weeks after moving to L.A., her hopes and dreams were shattered. In her book *Shipwrecked in L.A.*, Christin shares about the four years after her shipwreck—until she finally found her way home. More than a compelling story about her life and work in Hollywood, Christin shares what she learned about embracing a new sense of self and purpose after all of her hopes and dreams crashed.

Shipwrecked in L.A.

978-0-89827-698-5
978-0-89827-699-2 (e-book)

Is There Life After Jaded?

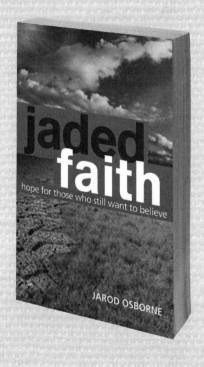

Many young adults are disillusioned with the faith they've inherited. They see the churches of their youth as superficial and irrelevant to their deepest concerns. Meanwhile, culture pushes and pulls them in many directions, none of its pathways leading to true life.

In *Jaded Faith*, Jarod Osborne confronts head-on the disorientation and disappointment you may be experiencing in your own journey of faith. He helps you navigate—spiritually and intellectually—the most common side-trails that cause young adults to wander from the Christian faith. You can find hope and life after jaded!

Jaded Faith

978-0-89827-570-4

978-0-89827-726-5 (e-book)